PIM1

12

POEMS FOR ALL PURPOSES

G. K. Chesterton (1874–1936) was born in London and lived there for more than half his life. He was educated at St Paul's School, at the Slade School of Art and at University College, London. He achieved greatness in most of the fields in which he earned his living – as a journalist, debater, broadcaster, and as the prolific author of both verse and prose. His fiction includes *The Napoleon of Notting Hill, The Man Who Was Thursday, Manalive* and *The Innocence of Father Brown*; he wrote biographies of G. F. Watts, Charles Dickens and St Thomas Aquinas; his incomparable essays are contained in *The Defendant, Lunacy and Letters* and a dozen other collections; of his travel books, *The New Jerusalem* is possibly the best; of his writings about his mental pilgrimage, the most influential are *Orthodoxy* and *The Everlasting Man*; and one of his articles in the *Illustrated London News* (1909) was responsible for Gandhi's concept of the true future for India.

Stephen Medcalf was educated at Chigwell School and Merton College, Oxford. He taught at Malvern College 1962–3 and, from the third year of its existence, at the University of Sussex, where he is now Reader in English in the School of European Studies. He has written on a wide range of subjects in thought and literature. He contributed an essay 'The Achievement of G. K. Chesterton' to *G. K. Chesterton: A Centenary Appraisal* (ed. John Sullivan, 1974) and has prepared an edition of *The Man Who Was Thursday*.

POEMS FOR ALL PURPOSES

The Selected Poems of
G. K. Chesterton

Edited and Introduced by
Stephen Medcalf

PIMLICO

PIMLICO

An imprint of Random House
20 Vauxhall Bridge Road, London SW1V 2SA

Random House Australia (Pty) Ltd
20 Alfred Street, Milsons Point, Sydney
New South Wales 2061, Australia

Random House New Zealand Ltd
18 Poland Road, Glenfield
Auckland 10, New Zealand

Random House South Africa (Pty) Ltd
PO Box 337, Bergvlei, South Africa

Random House UK Ltd Reg. No. 954009

This selection first published by Pimlico 1994

1 3 5 7 9 10 8 6 4 2

Introduction, notes and selection © Stephen Medcalf 1994

Printed and bound in Great Britain by
Clays Ltd, St Ives plc

ISBN 0–7126–5881–5

CONTENTS

INTRODUCTION

THE FLAG OF THE WORLD

'The world is not a lodging-house at Brighton, which we are to leave because it is miserable. It is the fortress of our family, with the flag flying on the turret, and the more miserable it is the less we should leave it . . .

Let us suppose we are confronted with a desperate thing – say Pimlico . . . It is not enough for a man to disapprove of Pimlico: in that case he will merely cut his throat or move to Chelsea. Nor, certainly, is it enough for a man to approve of Pimlico; for then it will remain Pimlico, which would be awful. The only way out of it seems to be for somebody to love Pimlico; to love it with a transcendental tie and without any earthly reason. If there arose a man who loved Pimlico, then Pimlico would rise into ivory towers and golden pinnacles; Pimlico would attire herself as a woman does when she is loved . . . Men did not love Rome because she was great. She was great because they had loved her . . .

I had found this hole in the world: the fact that one must somehow find a way of loving the world without trusting it . . .'

G. K. Chesterton, *Orthodoxy*, chapter V, 'The Flag of the World'

Aeschylus says that when the Greeks and Persians were about to join battle at Salamis, a voice cried to the Greeks, 'Now the fight is for everything.' Chesterton might have chosen these words as the motto for all his poetry. He believed that there was a need to fight for everything against nothing, for reality against illusion, for existence against suicide, for waking against nightmare, for sanity against despair. It was because these were his causes that he could reconcile the two poles in himself, that he was at once an unusually humble and gentle person, and furiously combative.

When he was at St Paul's School and his closest friend was Ed-mund Clerihew Bentley, who invented the clerihew there, he was already writing superb nonsense verse (some of it comes in the story of *The Taming of the Nightmare*), which suggests a hyperactive mind sitting loose to the world about him. It was perhaps having this kind of mind in the nihilistic atmosphere, as it impressed him, of Impressionism and Decadence at the Slade School of Art, between 1892 and 1894, that drove him into a 'maddening horror of un-reality', a sense of the world compounded of solipsism, sadistic fantasy and diabolism.

The most nearly contemporary account we have of his emergence from this state comes from a letter which he wrote in the summer of 1894 to Bentley, the first of the three people – the others were Frances Blogg and Hilaire Belloc – whom, as his poetry acknow-ledges, he loved above all his friends:

Inwardly speaking, I have had a funny time. A meaningless fit of depression, taking the form of certain absurd psychological wor-ries, came upon me, and instead of dismissing it and talking to people, I had it out and went very far into the abysses, indeed. The result was that I found that things, when examined, necessarily *spelt* such a mystically satisfactory state of things, that without getting back to earth, I saw lots that made me certain it is all right. The vision is fading into common day now, and I am glad. The frame of mind was the reverse of gloomy, but it would not do for long. It is embarrassing, talking with God face to face, as a man speaketh to his friend.

Scattered through his prose writings are fragments that seem to refer to this experience or intuition. In his *Autobiography* Chester-ton describes it as the 'mystical theory . . . that even mere existence, reduced to its most primary limits, was extraordinary enough to be exciting'. In the same passage he associates it with subjectivity, 'a forgotten blaze or burst of astonishment at our own existence', but in *St Thomas Aquinas* with objectivity, 'that strangeness of things, which is the light in all poetry, and indeed in all art'. In *St Thomas Aquinas* also, however, he brings the two sides together in our earliest perceptions, saying that long before the child 'knows that grass is grass, or self is self, he knows that something is something'. In *The Poet and the Lunatics* he says that this surprise at existence depends on the realisation of being a creature among creatures, realising that the world 'came from outside ourselves'; but in his essay on the book of Job he says that if one could imagine the

[2]

Creator He too would appear 'astonished at the things He has Himself made'. In *St Francis of Assisi* Chesterton describes the creature sharing in the understanding of the Creator: 'the mystic who passes through the moment when there is nothing but God, does in some sense behold the beginningless beginnings in which there was nothing else. He not only appreciates everything but the nothing of which everything was made.'

The fullest description of Chesterton's religious viewpoint is given to the Bulgarian monk Michael, who in *The Ball and the Cross* is left by Professor Lucifer hanging from the cross above the dome of St Paul's. As he climbs down, he experiences a state which is neither hope, faith nor knowledge, yet complete and of the present, positive, a satisfaction. 'It seems almost as if there were some equality among things, some balance in all possible contingencies which we are not permitted to know lest we should learn indifference to good and evil, but which is sometimes shown to us for an instant as a last aid in our last agony.' In that instant it seemed as if the universe had been newly created for Michael, and when he emerged on to Ludgate Hill, his eye feasted on everything it fell on with the appetite of 'a boy eating buns. He relished the squareness of the houses; he liked their clean angles as if he had just cut them with a knife.'

At the end of 1900, Chesterton published in *The Wild Knight* the poems which expressed this vision, and in *Greybeards at Play* nonsense verses which express two corollaries of it: that joy is more fundamental than grief, 'the uproarious labour by which all things live', and that the healthy man is known from the lunatic because his minor acts are 'careless and causeless' (*Orthodoxy*, chapters IX and II). Except by a certain joyful violence of hyperbole and paradox, expressing wonder, neither book stood out from the verse of the nineties so far as rhythm, metre, handling of the meanings of words or auditory imagination went. Indeed, it differed so little that one experienced reviewer, James Douglas, thought that 'G. K. Chesterton' must be the pseudonym of a well-established but equally violent poet, John Davidson. But the gratitude for existence and the pictorial impressions of an almost heraldic universe, whose colours and shapes blazon it as God's creation, should have told Douglas otherwise. Chesterton in his *Autobiography* instances 'By the Babe Unborn' as expressing his 'mystical theory'. It shares with Davidson's 'Thirty Bob a Week' the conceit that we chose to live before we were born. But Davidson, with echoes of Darwin and Nietzsche, imagines his clerk at thirty bob a week as choosing the conditions for the struggle of existence – Chesterton sees the unborn child as longing to experience, not so much the wonder of the qualities that things have, for that he is already dreaming of, nor as Gerard Manley Hopkins would have said the wonder of their particularity, but the very fact of their existence.

Most of the poems in *The Wild Knight* elaborate on this intuition. But some develop a further element. John Sullivan in his *Bibliography* of Chesterton attributes his best-remembered poem 'The Donkey', to 1894. The fourfold movement in its verses is certainly a kind of contemplation which fits the vision of that year. First we have an imagination of creation as a kind of nightmare, and second the setting of the donkey in that nightmare, 'to touch the nerve of surprise', as Chesterton says of the grotesque in his book on Browning, 'and thus to draw attention to the intrinsically miraculous character of the object itself'. Third, reacting from this monstrous vision, we focus more accurately on the pathos of the beast; and finally are made capable by our renewed vision to receive the sense that the donkey points beyond itself, not to the nightmare which we imposed on it, but, through its own implicit, animal memory of triumphant shouts and palms, to Christ's entry into Jerusalem. The new kind of wonder in the last verse, wonder at the Incarnation as well as the Creation, may suggest that the poem was written a year or so later than 1894. For Chesterton says in his *Autobiography*, and implies in the dedication to his *Ballad of the White Horse*, that he did not begin to take Christianity seriously until 1896, when he met Frances Blogg and fell in love with her. Many of the poems in *The Wild Knight* are either about her, like 'A Certain Evening', or about both her and Christianity, like 'Joseph' or 'The Praise of Dust'. They were married on 28 June 1901.

At about the same time, his poetry changed character. *The Wild Knight* was made up of the specialised, aesthetically self-conscious kind of literature which, however varied it may be in its style and subject, implies that it needs no purpose to justify its existence beyond being a poem. When in 1935 Chesterton assisted Ernest Rhys in making an Everyman selection of his writings, the part called Poems was made up of the whole of *The Wild Knight*, good and indifferent together, and 'Lepanto'. This may suggest that he thought of the rest of his shorter verse as something other than poems. Part of the reason would be that in 1899, in preparation for his marriage, he had given up working for a publisher and become a full-time journalist. And when, somewhere about 1907, his friend Father O'Connor thought that their friendship had become close enough for him to press Chesterton 'to go in for Literature', Frances objected, 'You will not change Gilbert, you will only fidget him. He is bent on being a jolly journalist, to paint the town red, and he does not need style to do that. All he wants is buckets and buckets of red paint.'

Romantic though in many ways he was, his particular humility made it natural for Chesterton to abandon much sense of himself as a poet in the romantic sense, as a person almost holy because inspired. Poetry became for him a craft, as it was for the mediaevals, a craft in which his virtuosity greatly increased, but which he did not often think of as self-justifying. He wrote huge quantities of verse for entertainment, especially ballades; he wrote hymns; he wrote political satires; he wrote for any purpose that required pointed speech.

In all this variety of verse, he did not lose his foundation in his mystical theory of existence. But there was a shift in expression here too. Whereas in *The Wild Knight* he presents the vision outright, and only occasionally (as in 'The Donkey') evokes or allows validity to the chaos and pessimism which is its background, later he creates within each poem an image of extreme desperation out of which the world can be created again. In his Christmas poems it is the despair of the pagan world and its 'mad gods' before the birth of God; in the 'Ballade of Suicide' it is the waiting gallows; often it is a war and a moment of clear defeat. His novels follow the same pattern, and their stories are commonly built round the epiphany of value out of defeat. In *The Man Who Was Thursday*, such a story is accompanied by a dedicatory ode to Bentley explaining it as an allegory of the crisis they shared in the nineties.

It is tempting to argue, from this sense that his struggle out of chaos had become a matter of memory, that with his marriage and acceptance of Christianity his inner difficulties were settled, and that this helps to account for his inclination after *The Wild Knight* to treat poetry as a craft rather than an art. For, as Yeats said, we make poetry out of our quarrel with ourselves, and rhetoric out of our quarrel with the world. This is very much a post-mediaeval contrast:

[5]

it would hardly have made sense to Chaucer or Langland. That it does not quite make sense for Chesterton either, is largely due to his somewhat mediaeval tendency to use allegory, which bridges the gap between world and self. We have seen it not only in relation to his imagery of crisis, but also in the heraldic nature of his visual imagination. Like Ewan Maclan in *The Ball and the Cross*, he tends to see a world in which everything is transparent: such as is 'figured in the coloured windows of Christian architecture'.

Chestertonian allegory is not of the kind in which concrete images mean abstractions. Meaning and value for him point to the personal or the particular, as in the 'Ballade of Suicide', where the answer to despair is a series of details so various as to discourage any generalisation. He constantly resolves his mystical theory of the excitingness of mere existence either into such details, or into the creed announced in *Orthodoxy*: 'that God was personal, and had made a world separate from Himself'. In that polarity, too, one must remember on the one hand that, because of His personality, as Chesterton says in his *Blake*, 'God is not a symbol of goodness. Goodness is a symbol of God', and on the other that the separateness of the world from God is what enables one to be loyal to it in the same complex way as one is loyal to something as particular as one's own home. It is in this creed that Chesterton finds what he was looking for in the passage quoted at the head of this essay, the way to love the world without trusting it: and it is this that he symbolises by the flag of the world. 'On this system one could fight all the forces of existence without deserting the flag of existence.'

Chesterton states here a subtle, and I believe true, way of distinguishing between an abstraction, which is general and impersonal, and a spirit, which is particular and personal. But its very subtlety makes it difficult to apply to the epiphanies of spirit in particular and concrete things. In Chesterton, the difficulty coincides with his personal difficulty of holding in polarity his humility and his combativeness.

The tensions involved may have been made more powerful, or simply more difficult, by his friendship with Hilaire Belloc, which began in 1900. In Belloc he encountered someone very like himself, but decidedly nearer the poles of combativeness and concern for the particular and concrete. One can see something of the consequence in *The Napoleon of Notting Hill*, which he dedicated to Belloc in 1904. The quality of the story is concentrated in a poem at once comic and tragic, the 'Anthem for the Feast of the Lamps', which, like *The Man Who Was Thursday*, expresses a moment of crisis – 'When the old guard of God turned to bay.' The dedicatory poem actualises this in terms of an historic war where fortunately Chesterton and Belloc could agree in admiring the particular loyalties of at least some people on both sides (that is the army of Napoleon and the fleet of Nelson). The overall message, that value in general is intimately connected with local loyalty in particular, and local loyalty with the willingness to fight, remains relatively untarnished.

The difficulty is greater with Belloc's anti-Semitism, although in this again Chesterton's humanity enabled him to escape by the skin of his teeth. Before 1933 he was apt to make one type of rich and politically powerful villain Jewish, as with Dr Gluck in *The Flying Inn* and the song which comes from it, 'The Logical Vegetarian'. In Edwardian England it was funny, even if coarse, to mock a figure like Dr Gluck, diplomatic representative of the German Empire, by rhyming 'vegetarian' with 'His attitudes were anything but Aryan'. In 1933, Chesterton's siding with the Jews as the powerless party was immediate, and his mockery of the fictitious Dr Gluck was paid for by his satire on the real General Goering and the notion of 'an Aryan people', in his poem 'Perfection'.

Some of his best satire attacks the misapplication of a loyalty or a principle, such as the identification of virtue with racial purity. His supreme achievement in this genre is 'Antichrist, or the Reunion of Christendom'. The point at issue is the way in which Christianity, which transcends nations, should be expressed among nations. F. E. Smith made a silly remark about the proposed disestablishment of the Anglican church in Wales. Establishment is the Anglican theory that Christianity should be expressed in human society as a set of distinct bodies, one in each distinct nation, holding a privileged position in it. Smith's silliness consisted in supposing that because Christianity transcends nations, the particular way in which it is expressed in Wales will be a matter of conscience in every Christian community in Europe. Chesterton's demolition of him is the funnier in proportion to its accuracy. But the difficulty of making such accurate judgments about epiphanies of the spirit in concrete things is illustrated by the fact that Chesterton would probably not have made the poem so funny if he had written it ten years later, when he had adopted the same view as Belloc's about the expression of Christianity in society, namely that its transcendence of nation can be expressed only in a concrete trans-national society, in the Roman Catholic Church. For the effect of the poem rests largely on its specification among the unWelsh parts of Christendom of various exotic but undoubtedly Christian Communities in Turkey and Russia which are no more Roman Catholic than they are Welsh. After 1922, Chesterton's Bellocian Catholicism would almost certainly not have allowed him to mention them.

Part of what attracted Chesterton in Christianity was that it allows 'opposite passions' to 'blaze beside each other', as he says in *Orthodoxy*: in particular, the opposite principles we have identified in him, violence and gentleness, he sees united in Christ. What he hoped for in his own poetry, it is reasonable to say, was an approximation to what he thought was the explanation of Christ's language, 'that it is the survey of one who from some supernatural height beholds some more startling synthesis'. He perhaps came closest to achieving it in the message given by Christ's mother in *The Ballad of the White Horse*:

> I tell you naught for your comfort,
>   Yea, naught for your desire,
> Save that the sky grows darker yet
>   And the sea rises higher.
>
> Night shall be thrice night over you,
>   And heaven an iron cope.
> Do you have joy without a cause,
>   Yea, Faith without a hope?

The Ballad of the White Horse draws together many of Chesterton's concerns. The White Horse itself is a more particular image of the flag of the world: partly because of personal associations going back to a memory from earliest childhood, of a white hobby-horse in a long upper room filled with light, and renewed because he began his honeymoon at the White Horse in Ipswich, but more because of the chalk cutting of the White Horse at Uffington. There are two principal theories about this figure: first, that it is a tribal emblem of Celts from the first century B.C., whose coins show a somewhat similar figure; and second, that it is a Saxon emblem, cut, as indeed local tradition maintains, by Alfred to commemorate his defeat of the Danes. Chesterton characteristically unites the two by supposing that Alfred restored the already immemorially old White Horse as an emblem of his restoration of civilisation. (He also, equally characteristically, unites the White Horse of Uffington, which may be associated with Alfred's fruitless victory against the Danes at Ashdown in 871, alluded to at the beginning of Book IV, with the White Horse of Westbury, which is close to the site of the battle of the poem at Ethandune or Edington in 878, but is not known to be older than the eighteenth century.)

The germ of the poem, however, was concerned with neither Alfred nor the White Horse, but with yet another personal myth of war, defeat and faith. At Battersea in the first years of Chesterton's marriage, probably in 1902 or 1903, some lines came to him in a dream:

> People, if you have any prayers
>   Say prayers for me.
> And bury me underneath a stone
>   In the stones of Battersea.

> Bury me underneath a stone,
>   With the sword that was my own;
> To wait till the holy horn is blown
>   And all poor men are free.

Presently, a little altered, these lines became Alfred's speech before the attack on the Danes. Father O'Connor remembered hearing the vision of the Virgin Mary, presumably including her message, on the first occasion when he met the Chestertons, in 1903 or 1904. The ballad grew by fragments until July 1910, when Chesterton travelled with Frances to the country of Alfred's struggle, and drew the whole thing together in a fortnight. It is in fact the literary work of his life which he took most time over. Yet when it was published, it contained one gross error – making the left wing of one army face the left wing of the other – which, although it was at once pointed out to him, Chesterton never corrected through a number of reprintings, until it was changed in the *Collected Poems*. And, even in the *Collected Poems*, the *Ballad* retains, alongside many splendours, the appalling self-parody of:

[9]

the hands of the happy howling men
　　　　Fling wide the gates of war.

The *Ballad* is a threefold allegory – history, legend, symbol. Taken as history, it is a plausible guess at the character of Alfred, who translated Boethius' *Consolation of Philosophy*, and at a point where the text seems to be affirming fatalism adds his own note, which Chesterton originally put at the head of the poem: 'I say, as do all Christian men, that it is a divine purpose that rules, and not Fate.' Taken as legend, it presents Chesterton's ideal of England – known in the Middle Ages as Mary's Dower – as the union of Roman, Saxon, Celt and Dane, representing law, homeliness, imagination and converted warlikeness. Taken as symbol it recapitulates his own struggles of the nineties, the Danish chieftains proclaiming philosophies which come closer and closer to his own misgivings, the amoral faith in racial destiny of Harold, Elf's awareness that 'there is always a thing forgotten/When all the world goes well', Ogier's nihilism and Guthrum's fatalism. Over against all four is Alfred's mystical faith in existence, that 'by God's death the stars shall stand/And the small apples grow'.

In the battle, legend and symbol join together. Harold is defeated by the Celt, Elf by the logic and discipline of Rome, but Ogier and Guthrum destroy all Alfred's followers and defeat him. But Mary has given him from her supernatural height the synthesis which is the basis of everything, and in the bottom of his defeat he shares the monk Michael's awareness of a balance in all possible contingencies. He wins, at the level of story because the Danes thought that the battle was over, at the level of symbol because he does not desert the flag of existence.

There follows from this moral what Guthrum in the end accepts – that, in the long run, even his continued existence will depend on Alfred's faith, 'because it is only Christian men/Guard even heathen things'. Conversely, Alfred's victory is not so much that he defeats Ogier's nihilism, although he does, as that he converts Guthrum – in which symbol and legend converge with history.

Chesterton never again in his poems quite achieved this inclusiveness. He almost did in 1911 with 'Lepanto', which is in fact a finer poem, a poem whose interwovenness, brilliance and profundity in sound, image and sense can best be appreciated by undertaking the surprisingly easy task of learning it by heart. Father O'Connor gave him the story after a discussion at the Ladies' Debating Society in Leeds, in the late spring of 1911, on the theme that all wars were religious wars. In June, Hilaire Belloc and Chesterton's brother Cecil founded a newspaper, the *Eye Witness*, to fight against plutocracy and combat political corruption. Its very nature was an incitement to Chesterton to write the kind of battling poetry that he liked; among other poems he wrote 'Lepanto', to appear on the annivers- ary of the battle, 7 October. It was finished under the sort of pressure to which he responded well – with the postman saying that he had ten minutes to catch the train. Yet its greatness, as one would expect of him, is in achieving a polarity of stillness over against noise, colour and combat. Two things must have attracted him in what Father O'Connor told him of the battle: its religious nature (with the enemy Islam, which Chesterton always associated with fatalism, stressed by the unlikelihood of the Christian nations co-operating except under the one heroic leader, Don John of Austria) and the story that the Pope saw a vision of it at prayer. This vision provided him with an image for supernatural survey and synthesis, 'The secret window whence the world looks small and very dear', which he is enabled to extend by the fact of Cervantes' having fought in the battle, so that a vision of Don Quixote is superimposed on the vision of Don John of Austria, and something close to Michael's and Alfred's balance of all possible contingencies is revealed. And Cervantes' smile, which expresses this balance, supersedes the tyrannical smile of victory of the Soldan at the opening of the poem.

But there is no-one like Guthrum in the poem, no possibility of conversion, and therefore no-one, neither Don John, nor Cervantes nor the Pope, to match Alfred. And one is left feeling that this much more historical poem than the *White Horse* has left more out. In the marvellous lines about Don John's freeing of the captives, one becomes vaguely aware we are not being told that Christians as well as Turks used galley-slaves, and that, as Charles Williams observes in his essay on Chesterton in *Poetry at Present*, Don John himself profited from the sale of slaves after the battle.

The combativeness, the need to take sides in a battle, appears spontaneously to be displacing the inclusiveness in Chesterton, and this displacement was enormously encouraged by two events: his brother's involvement in the Marconi Scandal of 1912, and the outbreak of the 1914 war. From November 1914 until Easter 1915 he was near death, largely from heart-trouble, and one wonders if some spiritual crisis in the two poles of combat and gentleness was responsible. In 1916 he wrote the 'Ballad of St Barbara' about the Battle of the Marne, and this poem is in the end ruined by that crisis. Three stories are again told: the story of St Barbara, the story of the Marne, and a story of spiritual perception. St Barbara, the head of the poem tells us, is the patron saint of artillery and of those in danger of sudden death. Her story, which explains these qualities, tells of her Christianity, of her revealing it by having a third window, emblematic of the Trinity, made in the two-windowed tower in which she was imprisoned, of her father's martyring her, and of his punishment by a thunderbolt. So far as Chesterton's poem tells of French retreat, the third window and Barbara's martyrdom, we are brought steadily closer to the promise of a vision of the world from beyond the world. But just as the window opens on 'the other side of things', the vision of Alfred, of Michael, of St Francis of Assisi is snatched from us. There is no moment of defeat and crisis: the guns, which were silent during the retreat, were only waiting for the moment to exert their maximum power, and Barbara the martyred patron of those in danger of sudden death is horribly revealed as the patron of artillery, in an orgasmic passage of triumph and destruction – 'St Barbara of the Gunners, with her hand upon the gun.' The conversion of an enemy like Guthrum is beyond all conceiving in this poem – 'They are burst asunder in the midst.' The poem is queerly reminiscent, partly by sheer contrast, not only of *The Ballad of the White Horse* but also of Simone Weil's essay on the second World War 'A War of Religions', with its stress that God's presence in the world is infinitely small, like a pearl or a seed, but wholly transforming and decisive. I think Chesterton partly intended to say something like that, and at the end of the poem he reverts to 'an unknown thing, never to come again,/That opened like the eye of God . . .' But Simone Weil insisted that 'the enemy force was halted when our strength was non-existent' in 1940, while Chesterton in 1914 remained enamoured of force.

When 'The Ballad of St Barbara' was published in 1922 it had along with it one poem, 'A Second Childhood', recalling as movingly as anything he wrote the wonder of existence, and another, 'The

Sword of Surprise', which carries the counterbalancing wonder at oneself a significant stage further, in a prayer to be sundered from oneself in order to save oneself. Chesterton's sense of combat and division had certainly increased, and along with it his need in allegory to identify the right with the particular. His visit to Jerusalem in 1919–20 produced two poems in which the transparency of the world approaches crisis. Jerusalem renews the sense, even in its blossoms, of something at once 'terrible' and yet 'no stranger to your bosom than bluebells of an English wood', the original blaze of astonishment at existence. But, associated particularly it seems with the ancient steps that go up from below Gethsemane to the church of St Peter in Gallicantu, there is a further sense of 'The stages of one towering drama/Always ahead and out of sight'; and associated with the Golden Gate the sense that someone standing on the wall might be Christ. Any Christian is likely to feel this sense of particularity in symbol at Jerusalem: Chesterton seems to have carried it away with him in the need to make his commitment to Christianity particular by conversion to the church of Rome. The sense of himself in 'The Sword of Surprise' is perhaps associated: he said in a letter to Ronald Knox about his conversion that he wanted 'all the morbid life of the lonely mind of a living person with whom I have lived . . . to end well'. He commemorated the sense of beginning a life entirely made new, with the sonnet 'The Convert', written on the day in which he was received into the Roman Catholic Church.

Although he wrote relatively little poetry thereafter, some of it did receive new life. In 1926 he published a set of poems in praise of the Virgin Mary, some of which are unlike anything he had written before in their contemplative quality. He had always loved the paradoxes of the incarnation, and they cohered, it seemed, with his habit of renewing awareness of ordinary things by making them look momentarily monstrous. In his Christmas poetry as in his other poetry he had loved hyperbole, and asserted gorgeously or violently that in this mother and child we find God. But in the traditional titles of Mary he had to hand already enormous hyperboles. And in 'A Little Litany' he uses these to imagine how God might see the earth. The 'secret window' of 'Lepanto' becomes Mary as 'gate of heaven' through which God 'saw the earth'. And two of the most gorgeous of her titles become simply the way in which God as a child sees her body, looking up:

Or risen from play at your pale raiment's hem
    God, grown adventurous from all time's repose,
Of your tall body climbed the ivory tower
    And kissed upon your mouth the mystic rose.

Comparably, the doctrine of the assumption of Mary bodily into heaven is softened in 'Regina Angelorum' into a dream of her wandering 'into a strange country' which recalls Belloc's pastoral and agnostic poem about Sussex:

I shall go without companions,
    And with nothing in my hand;
I shall pass through many places
    That I cannot understand
Until I come to my own country,
    Which is a pleasant land.

Others of the poems in *The Queen of Seven Swords* show Chesterton at his old hyperbolic tricks, so that Mary is 'Wild as of old and weird and sweet' with the moon rhyming 'beneath her feet'. But these two are like the vision of the crowned Mary with her child given to Jof (a character with whom Chesterton would have liked to be compared) in Ingmar Bergman's *Seventh Seal*. The vision of Mary in *The Ballad of the White Horse* is prepared for by Alfred's memory of the illuminated manuscript, so that it remains what we should see if we could 'look through Alfred's eyes'. But in these two poems Chesterton presents a vision, as Bergman does, in light such as we know today and in the space governed by modern sense of space.

Those of his latest poems which have never been collected suggest that his commitment to Roman Catholicism pushed his verse from poetry towards rhetoric, as if Yeats were right after all about the quarrel with ourselves and our quarrel with the world. The three best all came in 1929 – 'Ubi Ecclesia', which describes the Christian Church as the Castle East of the Sun and West of the Moon in fairytale, 'The Pagans', which begins finely with a laudation of traditional Christianity:

The Four Saints strong about the bed,
    The God that dies above the door;

Such mysteries as might dwell with men,
  The secret like a stooping face
Dim but not distant; and the night
  Not of the abyss, but the embrace;

though it lapses into a surreal mess when it describes paganism, and
'To St Michael in Time of Peace', whose picture of the archangel
Michael at the crucifixion Fr. O'Connor (having given up the at-
tempt to make Chesterton a literary man) called 'one of the high-
water marks of religious contemplation':

When from the deeps a dying God astounded
  Angels and devils who do all but die
Seeing Him fallen where thou couldst not follow
  Seeing Him mounted where thou couldst not fly,
Hand on the hilt, thou hast halted all thy legions
  Waiting the Tetelestai and the acclaim
Swords that salute Him dead and everlasting
  God beyond God and greater than His Name.

But even these, despite their fine passages, seem laboured as whole
poems, and their rhythms exist more for the love of twang and
thump than to express their sense.

In contrast, Chesterton's best poems have a disarming inevitability
of sense and sound which persuades his readers that his fight for
everything is our fight too. Since his death, perhaps the noblest
tribute paid to him was the leading article in *The Times* of 13 June
1941, when the meeting in St James's Palace of the representatives of
nine European states occupied by the Nazis was reported in two
hundred words, followed by the two verses of Mary's message to
Alfred. I do not know if anyone publicly quoted at the time of the
Communist coup against Gorbachev the line 'Of what huge devils
hid the stars, yet fell at a pistol flash', but it fitted well enough. At
such extreme crises, the validity of Chesterton's sense of the world
and the usefulness of his poetry are apparent: this selection of his
poems, arranged in an approximation to their order of writing may
suggest their variety, their inclusiveness, his powers of development,
and his happiness.

BIBLIOGRAPHY

I have used in this introduction principally Maisie Ward's *Gilbert Keith Chesterton* originally published in 1944, with some assistance from her *Return to Chesterton* (both Sheed & Ward), and from the lives of Chesterton by Dudley Barker, Michael Coren and Michael Ffinch, together with Fr J. O'Connor's *Father Brown on Chesterton* (Burns, Oates & Washbourne).

The poems of Chesterton are contained in:
The First Clerihews, O.U.P., 1982
The Coloured Lands, Sheed & Ward, 1938
The Napoleon of Notting Hill, John Lane, 1904
The Collected Poems of G. K. Chesterton, 3rd edition, Methuen, 1933
The Queen of Seven Swords, Sheed & Ward, 1926
G K's A Miscellany, Rich & Cowan, 1934
Collected Nonsense and Light Verse, ed. Marie Smith, Xanadu, 1987
Greybeards at Play, R. Brimley Johnson, 1900, republished by Paul Elek, 1974

I have also cannibalised some phrases from my own essay 'The Achievement of G. K. Chesterton' in *G. K. Chesterton: A Centenary Appraisal*, edited by John Sullivan (Paul Elek 1974), and have made great use of John Sullivan's *Bibliography* (University of London Press, 1958).

I POEMS AT SCHOOL
BEFORE JULY 1892

Solomon
You can scarcely write less than a column on.
His very song
Was long.

The Spanish people think Cervantes
Equal to half a dozen Dantes;
An opinion resented most bitterly
By the people of Italy.

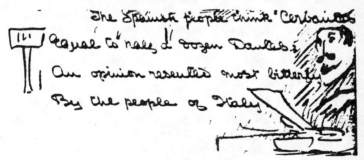

Thomas Carlyle
Has been forgotten all this while.
He wrote 'Sartor Resartus,'
But that shan't part us.

SONGS OF THE MOON CALF:
FROM *THE TAMING OF THE NIGHTMARE*

Jack clambered over the wall and entered the borderland of Creation.
Before he had gone far he came to a drop in the barren moors, which
showed him the broad pale face of the moon, ten times as large as
usual, and dark against it the lank melancholy figure of what looked
like an overgrown calf. He came nearer, and had to violently pull the
large animal's tail before he consented to take the least notice of his
presence. Then he slowly swung round, a large, pale, overgrown
head, with round rolling eyes, and looked abstractedly at the way-
farer. 'Can you tell me, where is the Mare's Nest?' asked Jack.

The Calf eyed him wistfully for a moment, and then replied in a
melancholy voice, with what appeared to be an impromptu rhyme of
doubtful relevancy!

> 'Oh, my limbs are very feeble,
> My head is very big,
> My ears are round, O do not, pray
> Mistake me for a pig.'

[22]

'Well, who wants to?' said the exasperated Horner. 'I only want to be directed.'

The Calf lifted his eyes to the moon a moment and then sang plaintively.

> 'This Calf was the Mooncalf, the Cow was the Moon,
> She died from effects of a popular tune,
> And now in her glory she shines in the sky;
> Oh, never had Calf such a mother as I.'

And so sweet and pathetic for the moment was the upward look of the poor monster that Jack was quite touched and forgot his own business and just stroked the lean ribs of the Mooncalf. And after a long pause there rose again from the creature the wild queer songs of worship.

> 'I forget all the creatures that taunt and despise,
> When through the dark night-mists my mother doth rise,
> She is tender and kind and she shines the night long
> On her lunatic child as he sings her his song.
> I was dropped on the dim earth to wander alone,
> And save this pale monster no child she hath known
> Without like on the earth, without sister or brother
> I sit here and sing to my mystical mother.'

And he sat there and sang for the remainder of the interview and as Jack, slowly and almost reluctantly, made his way onward over the dark moors, he could still hear the plaintive songs of the poetic Mooncalf rising, a solitary hum upon that gloomy waste, to the white moon overhead.

* * * *

> 'On thy poor offspring thy pale beams be given,
> Turning the dull moor to white halls of heaven,
> And in my songs, O Cow, from your memory slide off
> The painful effects of the tune that you died of.
> We sit here alone, but a joy to each other,
> The light to the child and the songs to the mother.'

II POEMS OF YOUTH
ca. 1894–ca. 1900

(i) POEMS PUBLISHED IN *THE WILD KNIGHT*, 1900

BY THE BABE UNBORN

[See Introduction.]

If trees were tall and grasses short,
  As in some crazy tale,
If here and there a sea were blue
  Beyond the breaking pale,

If a fixed fire hung in the air
  To warm me one day through,
If deep green hair grew on great hills,
  I know what I should do.

In dark I lie: dreaming that there
  Are great eyes cold or kind,
And twisted streets and silent doors,
  And living men behind.

Let storm-clouds come: better an hour,
  And leave to weep and fight,
Than all the ages I have ruled
  The empires of the night.

I think that if they gave me leave
  Within the world to stand,
I would be good through all the day
  I spent in fairyland.

They should not hear a word from me
  Of selfishness or scorn,
If only I could find the door,
  If only I were born.

THE SKELETON

Chattering finch and water-fly
Are not merrier than I;
Here among the flowers I lie
Laughing everlastingly.
No: I may not tell the best;
Surely, friends, I might have guessed
Death was but the good King's jest,
    It was hid so carefully.

ETERNITIES

I cannot count the pebbles in the brook.
    Well hath He spoken: 'Swear not by thy head,
    Thou knowest not the hairs,' though He, we read,
Writes that wild number in His own strange book.

I cannot count the sands or search the seas,
    Death cometh, and I leave so much untrod.
    Grant my immortal aureole, O my God,
And I will name the leaves upon the trees,

In heaven I shall stand on gold and glass,
    Still brooding earth's arithmetic to spell;
    Or see the fading of the fires of hell
Ere I have thanked my God for all the grass.

ECCLESIASTES

There is one sin: to call a green leaf grey,
    Whereat the sun in heaven shuddereth.
There is one blasphemy: for death to pray,
    For God alone knoweth the praise of death.

There is one creed: 'neath no world-terror's wing
    Apples forget to grow on apple-trees.
There is one thing is needful – everything –
    The rest is vanity of vanities.

Why should I care for the Ages
  Because they are old and grey?
To me, like sudden laughter,
  The stars are fresh and gay;
The world is a daring fancy,
  And finished yesterday.

Why should I bow to the Ages
  Because they were drear and dry?
Slow trees and ripening meadows
  For me go roaring by,
A living charge, a struggle
  To escalade the sky.

The eternal suns and systems,
  Solid and silent all,
To me are stars of an instant,
  Only the fires that fall
From God's good rocket, rising
  On this night of carnival.

GOLD LEAVES

Lo! I am come to autumn,
  When all the leaves are gold;
Grey hairs and golden leaves cry out
  The year and I are old.

In youth I sought the prince of men,
  Captain in cosmic wars,
Our Titan, even the weeds would show
  Defiant, to the stars.

But now a great thing in the street
  Seems any human nod,
Where shift in strange democracy
  The million masks of God.

[29]

In youth I sought the golden flower
　　Hidden in wood or wold,
But I am come to autumn,
　　When all the leaves are gold.

KING'S CROSS STATION

This circled cosmos whereof man is god
　　Has suns and stars of green and gold and red,
And cloudlands of great smoke, that range o'er range
　　Far floating, hide its iron heavens o'erhead.

God! shall we ever honour what we are,
　　And see one moment ere the age expire,
The vision of man shouting and erect,
　　Whirled by the shrieking steeds of flood and fire?

Or must Fate act the same grey farce again,
　　And wait, till one, amid Time's wrecks and scars,
Speaks to a ruin here, 'What poet-race
　　Shot such cyclopean arches at the stars?'

THE MIRROR OF MADMEN

I dreamed a dream of heaven, white as frost,
The splendid stillness of a living host;
Vast choirs of upturned faces, line o'er line.
Then my blood froze; for every face was mine.

Spirits with sunset plumage throng and pass,
Glassed darkly in the sea of gold and glass.
But still on every side, in every spot,
I saw a million selves, who saw me not.

I fled to quiet wastes, where on a stone,
Perchance, I found a saint, who sat alone;
I came behind: he turned with slow, sweet grace,
And faced me with my happy, hateful face.

[30]

I cowered like one that in a tower doth bide,
Shut in by mirrors upon every side;
Then I saw, islanded in skies alone
And silent, one that sat upon a throne.

His robe was bordered with rich rose and gold,
Green, purple, silver out of sunsets old;
But o'er his face a great cloud edged with fire,
Because it covereth a world's desire.

But as I gazed, a silent worshipper,
Methought the cloud began to faintly stir;
Then I fell flat, and screamed with grovelling head,
'If thou hast any lightning, strike me dead!

'But spare a brow where the clean sunlight fell,
The crown of a new sin that sickens hell.
Let me not look aloft and see mine own
Feature and form upon the Judgment-throne.'

Then my dream snapped: and with a heart that leapt
I saw across the tavern where I slept,
The sight of all my life most full of grace,
A gin-damned drunkard's wan half-witted face.

THOU SHALT NOT KILL

I had grown weary of him; of his breath
And hands and features I was sick to death.
Each day I heard the same dull voice and tread;
I did not hate him: but I wished him dead.
And he must with his blank face fill my life –
Then my brain blackened, and I snatched a knife.

But ere I struck, my soul's grey deserts through
A voice cried, 'Know at least what thing you do.
This is a common man: knowest thou, O soul,
What this thing is? somewhere where seasons roll
There is some living thing for whom this man

Is as seven heavens girt into a span,
For some one soul you take the world away –
Now know you well your deed and purpose. Slay!'
Then I cast down the knife upon the ground
And saw that mean man for one moment crowned.
I turned and laughed: for there was no one by –
The man that I had sought to slay was I.

A CERTAIN EVENING

That night the whole world mingled,
  The souls were babes at play,
And angel danced with devil,
  And God cried, 'Holiday!'

The sea had climbed the mountain peaks
  And shouted to the stars
To come to play: and down they came
  Splashing in happy wars.

The pine grew apples for a whim,
  The cart-horse built a nest;
The oxen flew, the flowers sang,
  The sun rose in the west.

And 'neath the load of many worlds,
  The lowest life God made
Lifted his huge and heavy limbs
  And into heaven strayed.

To where the highest life God made
  Before His presence stands;
But God Himself cried, 'Holiday!'
  And she gave me both her hands.

THE PRAISE OF DUST

'What of vile dust?' the preacher said.
  Methought the whole world woke,

The dead stone lived beneath my foot,
    And my whole body spoke.

'You, that play tyrant to the dust,
    And stamp its wrinkled face,
This patient star that flings you not
    Far into homeless space.

'Come down out of your dusty shrine
    The living dust to see,
The flowers that at your sermon's end
    Stand blazing silently.

'Rich white and blood-red blossom; stones,
    Lichens like fire encrust;
A gleam of blue, a glare of gold,
    The vision of the dust.

'Pass them all by: till, as you come
    Where, at the city's edge,
Under a tree – I know it well –
    Under a lattice ledge,

'The sunshine falls on one brown head.
    You, too, O cold of clay,
Eater of stones, may haply hear
    The trumpets of that day,

'When God to all his paladins
    By his own splendour swore
To make a fairer face than heaven,
    Of dust and nothing more.'

JOSEPH

If the stars fell; night's nameless dreams
    Of bliss and blasphemy came true,
If skies were green and snow were gold,
    And you loved me as I love you;

[33]

O long light hands and curled brown hair,
  And eyes where sits a naked soul;
Dare I even then draw near and burn
  My fingers in the aureole?

Yes, in the one wise foolish hour
  God gives this strange strength to a man.
He can demand, though not deserve,
  Where ask he cannot, seize he can.

But once the blood's wild wedding o'er,
  Were not dread his, half dark desire,
To see the Christ-child in the cot,
  The Virgin Mary by the fire?

A CHRISTMAS CAROL

The Christ-child lay on Mary's lap,
  His hair was like a light.
(O weary, weary were the world,
  But here is all aright.)

The Christ-child lay on Mary's breast,
  His hair was like a star.
(O stern and cunning are the kings,
  But here the true hearts are.)

The Christ-child lay on Mary's heart,
  His hair was like a fire.
(O weary, weary is the world,
  But here the world's desire.)

The Christ-child stood at Mary's knee,
  His hair was like a crown,
And all the flowers looked up at Him,
  And all the stars looked down.

When fishes flew and forests walked
    And figs grew upon thorn,
Some moment when the moon was blood
    Then surely I was born.

With monstrous head and sickening cry
    And ears like errant wings,
The devil's walking parody
    On all four-footed things.

The tattered outlaw of the earth,
    Of ancient crooked will;
Starve, scourge, deride me: I am dumb,
    I keep my secret still.

Fools! For I also had my hour;
    One far fierce hour and sweet:
There was a shout about my ears,
    And palms before my feet.

AN APOLOGY

Another tattered rhymster in the ring,
With but the old plea to the sneering schools,
That on him too, some secret night in spring,
Came the old frenzy of a hundred fools

To make some thing; the old want dark and deep,
The thirst of men, the hunger of the stars,
Since first it tinged even the Eternal's sleep,
With monstrous dreams of trees and towns and wars,

When all He made for the first time He saw,
Scattering stars as misers shake their pelf.
Then in the last strange wrath broke his own law,
And made a graven image of Himself.

A DEDICATION

TO E.C.B.

[Edmund Clerihew Bentley: see Introduction.]

He was, through boyhood's storm and shower,
   My best, my nearest friend;
We wore one hat, smoked one cigar,
   One standing at each end.

We were two hearts with single hope,
   Two faces in one hood;
I knew the secrets of his youth;
   I watched his every mood.

The little things that none but I
   Saw were beyond his wont,
The streaming hair, the tie behind,
   The coat tails worn in front.

I marked the absent-minded scream,
   The little nervous trick
Of rolling in the grate, with eyes
   By friendship's light made quick.

But youth's black storms are gone and past,
   Bare is each aged brow;
And, since with age we're growing bald,
   Let us be babies now.

Learning we knew; but still to-day,
   With spelling-book devotion,
Words of one syllable we seek
   In moments of emotion.

Riches we knew; and well dressed dolls –
   Dolls living – who expressed
No filial thoughts, however much
   You thumped them in the chest.

Old happiness is grey as we,
  And we may still outstrip her;
If we be slippered pantaloons,
  Oh let us hunt the slipper!

The old world glows with colours clear;
  And if, as saith the saint,
The world is but a painted show,
  Oh let us lick the paint!

Far, far behind are morbid hours,
  And lonely hearts that bleed.
Far, far behind us are the days,
  When we were old indeed.

Leave we the child: he is immersed
  With scientists and mystics:
With deep prophetic voice he cries
  Canadian food statistics.

But now I know how few and small,
  The things we crave need be –
Toys and the universe and you –
  A little friend to tea.

Behold the simple sum of things,
  Where, in one splendour spun,
The stars go round the Mulberry Bush,
  The Burning Bush, the Sun.

Now we are old and wise and grey,
  And shaky at the knees;
Now is the true time to delight
  In picture books like these.

Hoary and bent I dance one hour:
  What though I die at morn?
There is a shout among the stars,
  'To-night a child is born.'

I love to see the little stars
All dancing to one tune;
I think quite highly of the Sun,
And kindly of the Moon.

The million forests of the Earth
Come trooping in to tea.
The great Niagara waterfall
Is never shy with me.

I am the tiger's confidant,
　And never mention names:
The lion drops the formal 'Sir,'
　And lets me call him James.

Into my ear the blushing Whale
　Stammers his love. I know
Why the Rhinoceros is sad,
　– Ah, child! 'twas long ago.

I am akin to all the Earth
    By many a tribal sign:
The aged Pig will often wear
    That sad, sweet smile of mine.

My niece, the Barnacle, has got
    My piercing eyes of black;
The Elephant has got my nose,
    I do not want it back.

I know the strange tale of the Slug;
   The Early Sin – the Fall –
The Sleep – the Vision – and the Vow –
   The Quest – the Crown – the Call.

And I have loved the Octopus,
   Since we were boys together.
I love the Vulture and the Shark:
   I even love the weather.

I love to bask in sunny fields,
　And when that hope is vain,
I go and bask in Baker Street,
　All in the pouring rain.

Come snow! where fly, by some strange law,
　Hard snowballs – without noise –
Through streets untenanted, except
　By good unconscious boys.

Come fog! exultant mystery –
    Where, in strange darkness rolled,
The end of my own nose becomes
    A lovely legend old.

Come snow, and hail, and thunderbolts,
    Sleet, fire, and general fuss;
Come to my arms, come all at once –
    Oh photograph me thus!

(iii) THE NATIVITY

[Published December 1897 (*Parents' Review*) and revised
January 1902 (*Commonwealth*).]

The thatch on the roof was as golden,
  Though dusty the straw was and old,
The wind had a peal as of trumpets,
  Though blowing and barren and cold,
The mother's hair was a glory
  Though loosened and torn,
For under the eaves in the gloaming
  A child was born.

Have a myriad children been quickened,
  Have a myriad children grown old,
Grown gross and unloved and embittered,
  Grown cunning and savage and cold?
God abides in a terrible patience,
  Unangered, unworn,
And again for the child that was squandered
  A child is born.

What know we of aeons behind us,
  Dim dynasties lost long ago,
Huge empires, like dreams unremembered,
  Huge cities for ages laid low?
This at least – that with blight and with blessing,
  With flower and with thorn,
Love was there, and his cry was among them,
  'A child is born.'

Though the darkness be noisy with systems,
  Dark fancies that fret and disprove,
Still the plumes stir around us, above us
  The wings of the shadow of love:
Oh! princes and priests, have ye seen it
  Grow pale through your scorn;
Huge dawns sleep before us, deep changes,
  A child is born.

And the rafters of toil still are gilded
  With the dawn of the stars of the heart,
And the wise men draw near in the twilight,
  Who are weary of learning and art,
And the face of the tyrant is darkened,
  His spirit is torn,
For a new king is enthroned; yea, the sternest,
  A child is born.

And the mother still joys for the whispered
  First stir of unspeakable things,
Still feels that high moment unfurling
  Red glory of Gabriel's wings.
Still the babe of an hour is a master
  Whom angels adorn,
Emmanuel, prophet, anointed,
  A child is born.

And thou, that art still in thy cradle,
  The sun being crown for thy brow,
Make answer, our flesh, make an answer,
  Say, whence art thou come – who art thou?
Art thou come back on earth for our teaching
  To train or to warn –?
Hush – how may we know? – knowing only
  A child is born.

III FROM MARRIAGE TO THE WAR
ca. 1903–1914

(i) POEMS FOR ALL PURPOSES
ca. 1903–1909

[From *The Napoleon of Notting Hill*: Anthem commemorating the defence of Notting Hill in the battle of 3 October 1994. See Introduction. Published March 1904.]

When the world was in the balance, there was night on Notting Hill,
(There was night on Notting Hill): it was nobler than the day;
On the cities where the lights are and the firesides glow,
From the seas and from the deserts came the thing we did not know,
Came the darkness, came the darkness, came the darkness on the foe,
      And the old guard of God turned to bay.
For the old guard of God turns to bay, turns to bay,
And the stars fall down before it ere its banners fall to-day.
For when armies were around us as a howling and a horde,
When falling was the citadel and broken was the sword,
The darkness came upon them like the Dragon of the Lord,
      When the old guard of God turned to bay.

TO HILAIRE BELLOC

The Dedication of *The Napoleon of Notting Hill*

For every tiny town or place
   God made the stars especially;
Babies look up with owlish face
   And see them tangled in a tree:
You saw a moon from Sussex Downs,
   A Sussex moon, untravelled still,
I saw a moon that was the town's,
   The largest lamp on Campden Hill.

Yea, Heaven is everywhere at home,
   The big blue cap that always fits,
And so it is (be calm; they come
   To goal at last, my wandering wits),
So is it with the heroic thing;
   This shall not end for the world's end,
And though the sullen engines swing,
   Be you not much afraid, my friend.

[49]

This did not end by Nelson's urn
   Where an immortal England sits –
Nor where your tall young men in turn
   Drank death like wine at Austerlitz.
And when the pedants bade us mark
   What cold mechanic happenings
Must come; our souls said in the dark,
   'Belike; but there are likelier things.'

Likelier across these flats afar,
   These sulky levels smooth and free,
The drums shall crash a waltz of war
   And Death shall dance with Liberty;
Likelier the barricades shall blare
   Slaughter below and smoke above,
And death and hate and hell declare
   That men have found a thing to love.

Far from your sunny uplands set
   I saw the dream; the streets I trod,
The lit straight streets shot out and met
   The starry streets that point to God;
The legend of an epic hour
   A child I dreamed, and dream it still,
Under the great grey water tower
   That strikes the stars on Campden Hill.

A BALLADE OF SUICIDE

[Published 21 August 1911, *Eye Witness*; but according to Fr O'Connor written 1903 or 1904. It was a convention of the ballades of Chesterton & his friends that the *Envoi* should insult the Prince. Germinal: Revolutionary name of the month in which the Terror began in France in 1793, although the Revolutionary names of the months were not in force until the following year.]

The gallows in my garden, people say,
Is new and neat and adequately tall.
I tie the noose on in a knowing way
As one that knots his necktie for a ball;
But just as all the neighbours – on the wall –

Are drawing a long breath to shout 'Hurray!'
The strangest whim has seized me . . . After all
I think I will not hang myself to-day.

To-morrow is the time I get my pay –
My uncle's sword is hanging in the hall –
I see a little cloud all pink and grey –
Perhaps the Rector's mother will *not* call –
I fancy that I heard from Mr. Gall
That mushrooms could be cooked another way –
I never read the works of Juvenal –
I think I will not hang myself to-day.

The world will have another washing day;
The decadents decay; the pedants pall;
And H. G. Wells has found that children play,
And Bernard Shaw discovered that they squall;
Rationalists are growing rational –
And through thick woods one finds a stream astray,
So secret that the very sky seems small –
I think I will not hang myself to-day.

Envoi
Prince, I can hear the trumpet of Germinal,
The tumbrils toiling up the terrible way;
Even to-day your royal head may fall –
I think I will not hang myself to-day.

TRANSLATION FROM DU BELLAY

['Heureux qui, comme Ullysse, a fait un beau voyage':
Published in *Occasional Papers*, July 1904.]

Happy, who like Ulysses or that lord
   Who raped the fleece, returning full and sage,
With usage and the world's wide reason stored,
   With his own kin can taste the end of age.
When shall I see, when shall I see, God knows!
   My little village smoke; or pass the door,

The old dear door of that unhappy house
  Which is to me a kingdom and much more?
Mightier to me the house my fathers made
  Than your audacious heads, O Halls of Rome!
More than immortal marbles undecayed,
  The thin sad slates that cover up my home;
More than your Tiber is my Loire to me,
  Than Palatine my little Lyré there;
And more than all the winds of all the sea
  The quiet kindness of the Angevin air.

FRAGMENT FROM DANTE

[*Paradiso* XXXIII, 49–78]

Then Bernard smiled at me, that I should gaze
  But I had gazed already; caught the view,
Faced the unfathomable ray of rays
  Which to itself and by itself is true.

Then was my vision mightier than man's speech;
  Speech snapt before it like a flying spell;
And memory and all that time can teach
  Before that splendid outrage failed and fell.

As when one dreameth and remembereth not
  Waking, what were his pleasures or his pains,
With every feature of the dream forgot,
  The printed passion of the dream remains:–

Even such am I; within whose thoughts resides
  No picture of that sight nor any part,
Nor any memory: in whom abides
  Only a happiness within the heart,

A secret happiness that soaks the heart
  As hills are soaked by slow unsealing snow,
Or secret as that wind without a chart
  Whereon did the wild leaves of Sibyl go.

[52]

O light uplifted from all mortal knowing,
  Send back a little of that glimpse of thee,
That of its glory I may kindle glowing
  One tiny spark for all men yet to be.

THE WISE MEN

[Published Christmas Day, 1905, *Daily News*]

Step softly, under snow or rain,
  To find the place where men can pray;
The way is all so very plain
  That we may lose the way.

Oh, we have learnt to peer and pore
  On tortured puzzles from our youth,
We know all labyrinthine lore,
We are the three wise men of yore,
  And we know all things but the truth.

We have gone round and round the hill
  And lost the wood among the trees,
And learnt long names for every ill,
And served the mad gods, naming still
  The furies the Eumenides.

The gods of violence took the veil
  Of vision and philosophy,
The Serpent that brought all men bale,
He bites his own accursed tail,
  And calls himself Eternity.

Go humbly . . . it has hailed and snowed . . .
  With voices low and lanterns lit;
So very simple is the road,
  That we may stray from it.

The world grows terrible and white,
  And blinding white the breaking day;
We walk bewildered in the light,

[53]

For something is too large for sight,
   And something much too plain to say.

The Child that was ere worlds begun
   (. . . We need but walk a little way,
We need but see a latch undone . . .)
The Child that played with moon and sun
   Is playing with a little hay.

The house from which the heavens are fed,
   The old strange house that is our own,
Where tricks of words are never said,
And Mercy is as plain as bread,
   And Honour is as hard as stone.

Go humbly, humble are the skies,
   And low and large and fierce the Star;
So very near the Manger lies
   That we may travel far.

Hark! Laughter like a lion wakes
   To roar to the resounding plain,
And the whole heaven shouts and shakes,
For God Himself is born again,
And we are little children walking
   Through the snow and rain.

THE HOUSE OF CHRISTMAS

[Published in *A Chesterton Calendar*, January 1911;
but like most things in the *Calendar*, probably written earlier.]

There fared a mother driven forth
Out of an inn to roam;
In the place where she was homeless
All men are at home.
The crazy stable close at hand,
With shaking timber and shifting sand,

Grew a stronger thing to abide and stand
Than the square stones of Rome.

For men are homesick in their homes,
And strangers under the sun,
And they lay their heads in a foreign land
Whenever the day is done.
Here we have battle and blazing eyes,
And chance and honour and high surprise,
But our homes are under miraculous skies
Where the yule tale was begun.

A Child in a foul stable,
Where the beasts feed and foam;
Only where He was homeless
Are you and I at home;
We have hands that fashion and heads that know,
But our hearts we lost – how long ago!
In a place no chart nor ship can show
Under the sky's dome.

This world is wild as an old wives' tale,
And strange the plain things are,
The earth is enough and the air is enough
For our wonder and our war;
But our rest is as far as the fire-drake swings
And our peace is put in impossible things
Where clashed and thundered unthinkable wings
Round an incredible star.

To an open house in the evening
Home shall men come,
To an older place than Eden
And a taller town than Rome.
To the end of the way of the wandering star,
To the things that cannot be and that are,
To the place where God was homeless
And all men are at home.

A HYMN

[Published in *The English Hymnal*, 1906.]

O God of earth and altar,
  Bow down and hear our cry,
Our earthly rulers falter,
  Our people drift and die;
The walls of gold entomb us,
  The swords of scorn divide,
Take not thy thunder from us,
  But take away our pride.

From all that terror teaches,
  From lies of tongue and pen,
From all the easy speeches
  That comfort cruel men,
From sale and profanation
  Of honour and the sword,
From sleep and from damnation,
  Deliver us, good Lord.

Tie in a living tether
  The prince and priest and thrall,
Bind all our lives together,
  Smite us and save us all;
In ire and exultation
  Aflame with faith, and free,
Lift up a living nation,
  A single sword to thee.

THE SECRET PEOPLE

[Published in *The Neolith*, 1907.]

Smile at us, pay us, pass us; but do not quite forget;
For we are the people of England, that never have spoken yet.
There is many a fat farmer that drinks less cheerfully,
There is many a free French peasant who is richer and sadder than we.

There are no folk in the whole world so helpless or so wise.
There is hunger in our bellies, there is laughter in our eyes;
You laugh at us and love us, both mugs and eyes are wet:
Only you do not know us. For we have not spoken yet.

The fine French kings came over in a flutter of flags and dames.
We liked their smiles and battles, but we never could say their
    names.
The blood ran red to Bosworth and the high French lords went
    down;
There was naught but a naked people under a naked crown.
And the eyes of the King's Servants turned terribly every way,
And the gold of the King's Servants rose higher every day.
They burnt the homes of the shaven men, that had been quaint and
    kind,
Till there was no bed in a monk's house, nor food that man could
    find.
The inns of God where no man paid, that were the wall of the weak,
The King's Servants ate them all. And still we did not speak.

And the face of the King's Servants grew greater than the King:
He tricked them, and they trapped him, and stood round him in a
    ring.
The new grave lords closed round him, that had eaten the abbey's
    fruits,
And the men of the new religion, with their bibles in their boots,
We saw their shoulders moving, to menace or discuss,
And some were pure and some were vile; but none took heed of us.
We saw the King as they killed him, and his face was proud and
    pale;
And a few men talked of freedom, while England talked of ale.

A war that we understood not came over the world and woke
Americans, Frenchmen, Irish; but we knew not the things they
    spoke.
They talked about rights and nature and peace and the people's
    reign:
And the squires, our masters, bade us fight; and scorned us never
    again.

[57]

Weak if we be for ever, could none condemn us then;
Men called us serfs and drudges; men knew that we were men.
In foam and flame at Trafalgar, on Albuera plains,
We did and died like lions, to keep ourselves in chains
We lay in living ruins; firing and fearing not
The strange fierce face of the Frenchmen who knew for what they
    fought,
And the man who seemed to be more than man we strained against
    and broke;
And we broke our own rights with him. And still we never spoke.

Our patch of glory ended; we never heard guns again.
But the squire seemed struck in the saddle; he was foolish, as if in
    pain.
He leaned on a staggering lawyer, he clutched a cringing Jew,
He was stricken; it may be, after all, he was stricken at Waterloo.
Or perhaps the shades of the shaven men, whose spoil is in his
    house,
Come back in shining shapes at last to spoil his last carouse:
We only know the last sad squires ride slowly towards the sea,
And a new people takes the land: and still it is not we.

They have given us into the hand of new unhappy lords,
Lords without anger and honour, who dare not carry their swords.
They fight by shuffling papers; they have bright dead alien eyes;
They look at our labour and laughter as a tired man looks at flies.
And the load of their loveless pity is worse than the ancient wrongs,
Their doors are shut in the evening; and they know no songs.

We hear men speaking for us of new laws strong and sweet,
Yet is there no man speaketh as we speak in the street.
It may be we shall rise the last as Frenchmen rose the first,
Our wrath come after Russia's wrath and our wrath be the worst.
It may be we are meant to mark with our riot and our rest
God's scorn for all men governing. It may be beer is best.
But we are the people of England; and we have not spoken yet.
Smile at us, pay us, pass us. But do not quite forget.

A HYMN FOR THE CHURCH MILITANT

[Published November 1907 in *Commonwealth*.]

Great God, that bowest sky and star,
  Bow down our towering thoughts to thee,
And grant us in a faltering war
  The firm feet of humility.

Lord, we that snatch the swords of flame,
  Lord, we that cry about Thy car,
We too are weak with pride and shame,
  We too are as our foemen are.

Yea, we are mad as they are mad,
  Yea, we are blind as they are blind,
Yea, we are very sick and sad
  Who bring good news to all mankind.

The dreadful joy Thy Son has sent
  Is heavier than any care;
We find, as Cain his punishment,
  Our pardon more than we can bear.

Lord, when we cry Thee far and near
  And thunder through all lands unknown
The gospel into every ear,
  Lord, let us not forget our own.

Cleanse us from ire of creed or class,
  The anger of the idle kings;
Sow in our souls, like living grass,
  The laughter of all lowly things.

THE CHRISTIAN SOCIAL UNION

[Records a meeting in Nottingham: reconstructed from Chesterton's *Autobiography* and Fr John O'Connor's *Father Brown on Chesterton*. Exact date uncertain.]

The Christian Social Union here
Was very much annoyed;
It seems there is some duty
Which we never should avoid,
And so they sang a lot of hymns
To help the Unemployed.

Upon a platform at the end
The speakers were displayed
And Bishop Hoskins stood in front
And hit a bell and said
That Mr. Carter was to pray,
And Mr. Carter prayed.

Then Bishop Gore of Birmingham
He stood upon one leg
And said he would be happier
If beggars didn't beg,
And that if they pinched his palace
It would take him down a peg.

He said that Unemployment
Was a horror and a blight,
He said that charities produced
Servility and spite,
And stood upon the other leg
And said it wasn't right.

And then a man named Chesterton
Got up and played with water,
He seemed to say that principles
Were nice and led to slaughter
And how we always compromised
And how we didn't orter.

Then Canon Holland fired ahead
Like fifty cannons firing,
We tried to find out what he meant
With infinite enquiring,
But the way he made the windows jump
We couldn't help admiring.

I understood him to remark
(It seemed a little odd)
That half a dozen of his friends
Had never been in quod.
He said he was a Socialist
Himself, and so was God.

He said the human soul should be
Ashamed of every sham,
He said a man should constantly
Ejaculate 'I am.'
When he had done, I went outside
And got into a tram.

TO EDMUND CLERIHEW BENTLEY

The Dedication of *The Man Who Was Thursday*

[Published February 1908: see Introduction. Of the two giants, the first is Walt Whit-
man: 'fish-shaped Paumanok' is his birthplace, Long Island, and refers to a poem in
his *Leaves of Grass*. Tusitala is R. L. Stevenson; the green carnation the emblem of
Oscar Wilde.]

A cloud was on the mind of men, and wailing went the weather,
Yea, a sick cloud upon the soul when we were boys together.
Science announced nonentity and art admired decay;
The world was old and ended: but you and I were gay.
Round us in antic order their crippled vices came –
Lust that had lost its laughter, fear that had lost its shame.
Like the white lock of Whistler, that lit our aimless gloom,
Men showed their own white feather as proudly as a plume.
Life was a fly that faded, and death a drone that stung;
The world was very old indeed when you and I were young.

They twisted even decent sin to shapes not to be named:
Men were ashamed of honour; but we were not ashamed.
Weak if we were and foolish, not thus we failed, not thus;
When that black Baal blocked the heavens he had no hymns from us.
Children we were – our forts of sand were even as weak as we,
High as they went we piled them up to break that bitter sea.
Fools as we were in motley, all jangling and absurd,
When all church bells were silent our cap and bells were heard.
Not all unhelped we held the fort, our tiny flags unfurled;
Some giants laboured in that cloud to lift it from the world.
I find again the book we found, I feel the hour that flings
Far out of fish-shaped Paumanok some cry of cleaner things;
And the Green Carnation withered, as in forest fires that pass,
Roared in the wind of all the world ten million leaves of grass;
Or sane and sweet and sudden as a bird sings in the rain –
Truth out of Tusitala spoke and pleasure out of pain.
Yea, cool and clear and sudden as a bird sings in the grey,
Dunedin to Samoa spoke, and darkness unto day.
But we were young; we lived to see God break their bitter charms,
God and the good Republic come riding back in arms:
We have seen the city of Mansoul, even as it rocked, relieved –
Blessed are they who did not see, but being blind, believed.

This is a tale of those old fears, even of those emptied hells,
And none but you shall understand the true thing that it tells –
Of what colossal gods of shame could cow men and yet crash,
Of what huge devils hid the stars, yet fell at a pistol flash.
The doubts that were so plain to chase, so dreadful to withstand –
Oh, who shall understand but you; yea, who shall understand?
The doubts that drove us through the night as we two talked amain,
And day had broken on the streets e'er it broke upon the brain.
Between us, by the peace of God, such truth can now be told;
Yea, there is strength in striking root, and good in growing old.
We have found common things at last, and marriage and a creed,
And I may safely write it now, and you may safely read.

POEMS WRITTEN ON HOLIDAY

THE BALLADE OF A STRANGE TOWN

[Published in the *Daily News*, 2 May 1908.]

My friend and I, in fooling about Flanders fell into a fixed affection for the town of Mechlin or Malines. Our rest there was so restful that we almost felt it as a home, and hardly strayed out of it.

We sat day after day in the market-place, under little trees growing in wooden tubs, and looked up at the noble converging lines of the Cathedral tower, from which the three riders from Ghent, in the poem, heard the bell which told them they were not too late. But we took as much pleasure in the people, in the little boys with open, flat Flemish faces and fur collars round their necks, making them look like burgo-masters; or the women, whose prim, oval faces, hair strained tightly off the temples, and mouths at once hard, meek, and humorous, exactly reproduced the late medieval faces in Memling and Van Eyck.

But one afternoon, as it happened, my friend rose from under his little tree, and, pointing to a sort of toy train that was puffing smoke in one corner of the clear square, suggested that we should go by it. We got into the little train, which was meant really to take the peasants and their vegetables to and fro from their fields beyond the town, and the official came round to give us tickets. We asked him what place we should get to if we paid fivepence. The Belgians are not a romantic people, and he asked us (with a lamentable mixture of Flemish coarseness and French rationalism) where we wanted to go.

We explained that we wanted to go to fairyland, and the only question was whether we could get there for fivepence. At last, after a great deal of international misunderstanding (for he spoke French in the Flemish and we in the English manner), he told us that fivepence would take us to a place which I have never seen written down, but which when spoken sounded like the word 'Waterloo' pronounced by an intoxicated patriot; I think it was Waerlowe. We clasped our hands and said it was the place that we had been seeking from boyhood, and when we had got there we descended with promptitude.

[63]

For a moment I had a horrible fear that it really was the field of Waterloo; but I was comforted by remembering that it was in quite a different part of Belgium. It was a cross-roads, with one cottage at the corner, a perspective of tall trees like Hobbema's 'Avenue', and beyond only the infinite flat chess-board of the little fields. It was the scene of peace and prosperity; but I must confess that my friend's first action was to ask the man when there would be another train back to Mechlin. The man stated that there would be a train back in exactly one hour. We walked up the avenue, and when we were nearly half an hour's walk away it began to rain.

We arrived back at the cross-roads sodden and dripping, and, finding the train waiting, climbed into it with some relief. The officer on this train could speak nothing but Flemish, but he understood the name of Mechlin, and indicated that when we came to Mechlin Station he would put us down, which, after the right interval of time, he did.

We got down, under a steady downpour, evidently on the edge of Mechlin, though the features could not easily be recognized through the grey screen of the rain. I do not generally agree with those who find rain depressing. A shower-bath is not depressing; it is rather startling. And if it is exciting when a man throws a pail of water over you, why should it not also be exciting when the gods throw many pails? But on this soaking afternoon, whether it was the dull sky-line of the Netherlands or the fact that we were returning home without any adventure, I really did think things a trifle dreary. As soon as we could creep under the shelter of a street we turned in to a little café, kept by one woman. She was incredibly old, and she spoke no French. There we drank black coffee and what was called 'cognac fine'. 'Cognac fine' were the only two French words used in the establishment, and they were not true. At least, the fineness (perhaps by its very ethereal delicacy) escaped me. After a little my friend, who was more restless than I, got up and went out, to see if the rain had stopped and if we could at once stroll back to our hotel by the station. I sat finishing my coffee in a colourless mood, and listening to the unremitting rain.

Suddenly the door burst open, and my friend appeared, transfigured and frantic.

'Get up!' he cried, waving his hands wildly. 'Get up! We're in the wrong town! We're not in Mechlin at all. Mechlin is ten miles, twenty miles off – God knows what! We're somewhere near Antwerp.'

'What!' I cried, leaping from my seat, and sending the furniture flying. 'Then all is well, after all! Poetry only hid her face for an instant behind a cloud. Positively for a moment I was feeling depressed because we were in the right town. But if we are in the wrong town – why, we have our adventure after all! If we are in the wrong town, we are in the right place.'

I rushed out into the rain, and my friend followed me somewhat more grimly. We discovered we were in a town called Lierre, which seemed to consist chiefly of bankrupt pastry-cooks who sold lemonade.

'This is the peak of our whole poetic progress!' I cried enthusiastically. 'We must do something, something sacramental and commemorative! We cannot sacrifice an ox, and it would be a bore to build a temple. Let us write a poem.'

With but slight encouragement, I took out an old envelope and one of those pencils that turn bright violet in water. There was plenty of water about, and the violet ran down the paper, symbolizing the rich purple of that romantic hour. I began, choosing the form of an old French ballade; it is the easiest because it is the most restricted:

'Can Man to Mount Olympus rise,
    And fancy Primrose Hill the scene?
Can a man walk in Paradise
    And think he is in Turnham Green?
And could I take you for Malines,
    Not knowing the nobler thing you were?
O Pearl of all the plain, and queen,
    The lovely city of Lierre.

'Through memory's mist in glimmering guise
    Shall shine your street of sloppy sheen.
And wet shall grow my dreaming eyes,
    To think how wet my boots have been.
Now if I die or shoot a Dean –'

Here I broke off to ask my friend whether he thought it expressed a more wild calamity to shoot a Dean or to be a Dean. But he only turned up his coat collar, and I felt that for him the muse had folded her wings. I re-wrote:

'Now if I die a Rural Dean,
　Or rob a bank I do not care,
Or turn a Tory. I have seen
　The lovely city of Lierre.'

'The next line,' I resumed warming to it; but my friend interrupted me.

'The next line,' he said somewhat harshly, 'will be a railway line. We can get back to Mechlin from here, I find, though we have to change twice. I dare say I should think this jolly romantic but for the weather. Adventure is the champagne of life, but I prefer my champagne and my adventures dry. Here is the station.'

We did not speak again until we had left Lierre, in its sacred cloud of rain, and were coming to Mechlin, under a clearer sky, that even made one think of stars. Then I leant forward and said to my friend in a low voice:

'I have found out everything. We have come to the wrong star.'

He stared his query, and I went on eagerly: 'That is what makes life at once so splendid and so strange. We are in the wrong world. When I thought that was the right town, it bored me; when I knew it was wrong, I was happy. So the false optimism, the modern happiness, tires us because it tells us we fit into this world. The true happiness is that we don't fit. We come from somewhere else. We have lost our way.'

He silently nodded, staring out of the window, but whether I had impressed or only fatigued him I could not tell. 'This,' I added, 'is suggested in the last verse of a fine poem you have grossly neglected:

' "Happy is he and more than wise
　Who sees with wondering eyes and clean
This world through all the grey disguise
　Of sleep and custom in between.

' "Yes; we may pass the heavenly screen,
     But shall we know when we are there?
 Who know not what these dead stones mean,
     The lovely city of Lierre." '

Here the train stopped abruptly. And from Mechlin church steeple
we heard the half-chime: and Joris broke silence with 'No bally *hors
d'œuvres* for me: I shall get on to something solid at once.'

L'Envoy
Prince, wide your Empire spreads, I ween,
     Yet happier is that moistened Mayor,
 Who drinks her cognac far from *fine*,
     The lovely city of Lierre.

THE LITTLE BIRDS WHO WON'T SING

[*Daily News*, 16 May 1908.]

On my last morning on the Flemish coast, when I knew that in a few
hours I should be in England, my eye fell upon one of the details of
Gothic carving of which Flanders is full. I do not know whether the
thing was old, though it was certainly knocked about and indeci-
pherable, but at least it was certainly in the style and tradition of the
early Middle Ages. It seemed to represent men bending themselves
(not to say twisting themselves) to certain primary employments.
Some seemed to be sailors tugging at ropes; others, I think, were
reaping; others were energetically pouring something into something
else. This is entirely characteristic of the pictures and carvings of the
early thirteenth century, perhaps the most purely vigorous time in all
history. The great Greeks preferred to carve their gods and heroes
doing nothing. Splendid and philosophic as their composure is there
is always about it something that marks the master of many slaves.
But if there was one thing the early medievals liked it was repres-
enting people doing something – hunting or hawking, or rowing
boats, or treading grapes, or making shoes, or cooking something
in a pot. 'Quicquid agunt homines votum timor ira voluptas.'
(I quote from memory.) The Middle Ages is full of that spirit in all
its monuments and manuscripts. Chaucer retains it in his jolly

[67]

insistence on everybody's type of trade and toil. It was the earliest and youngest resurrection of Europe, the time when social order was strengthening, but had not yet become oppressive; the time when religious faiths were strong, but had not yet been exasperated. For this reason the whole effect of Greek and Gothic carving is different. The figures in the Elgin marbles, though often rearing their steeds for an instant in the air, seem frozen for ever at that perfect instant. But a mass of medieval carving seems actually a sort of bustle or hubbub in stone. Sometimes one cannot help feeling that the groups actually move and mix, and the whole front of a great cathedral has the hum of a huge hive.

But about these particular figures there was a peculiarity of which I could not be sure. Those of them that had any heads had very curious heads, and it seemed to me that they had their mouths open. Whether or no this really meant anything or was an accident of nascent art I do not know; but in the course of wondering I recalled to my mind the fact that singing was connected with many of the tasks there suggested, that there were songs for reapers reaping and songs for sailors hauling ropes. I was still thinking about this small problem when I walked along the pier at Ostend; and I heard some sailors uttering a measured shout as they laboured, and I remembered that sailors still sing in chorus while they work, and even sing different songs according to what part of their work they are doing. And a little while afterwards, when my sea journey was over, the sight of men working in the English fields reminded me again that there are still songs for harvest and for many agricultural routines. And I suddenly wondered why if this were so it should be quite unknown for any modern trade to have a ritual poetry. How did people come to chant rude poems while pulling certain ropes or gathering certain fruit, and why did nobody do anything of the kind while producing any of the modern things? Why is a modern newspaper never printed by people singing in chorus? Why do shopmen seldom, if ever, sing?

If reapers sing while reaping, why should not auditors sing while auditing and bankers while banking? If there are songs for all the separate things that have to be done in a boat, why are there not songs for all the separate things that have to be done in a bank? As the train from Dover flew through the Kentish gardens, I tried to write a few songs suitable for commercial gentlemen. Thus, the work of bank clerks when casting up columns might begin with a thundering chorus in praise of Simple Addition.

'Up my lads, and lift the ledgers, sleep and ease are o'er.
   Hear the Stars of Morning shouting: "Two and Two are Four."
Though the creeds and realms are reeling, though the sophists roar,
   Though we weep and pawn our watches, Two and Two are Four.'

And then, of course, we should need another song for times of financial crisis and courage, a song with a more fierce and panic-stricken metre, like the rushing of horses in the night:

'There's a run upon the Bank –
         Stand away!
For the Manager's a crank and the Secretary drank, and the
   Upper Tooting Bank
         Turns to bay!
Stand close: there is a run
         On the Bank.
Of our ship, our royal one, let the ringing legend run, that she fired
   with every gun
         Ere she sank.'

And as I came into the cloud of London I met a friend of mine who actually is in a bank, and submitted these suggestions in rhyme to him for use among his colleagues. But he was not very hopeful about the matter. It was not (he assured me) that he underrated the verses, or in any sense lamented their lack of polish. No; it was rather, he felt, an indefinable something in the very atmosphere of the society in which we live that makes it spiritually difficult to sing in banks. And I think he must be right; though the matter is very mysterious. I may observe here that I think there must be some mistake in the calculations of the Socialists. They put down all our distress not to a moral tone, but to the chaos of private enterprise. Now, banks are private; but post offices are Socialistic: therefore I naturally expected that the post office would fall into the collectivist idea of a chorus. Judge of my surprise when the lady in my local post office (whom I urged to sing) dismissed the idea with far more coldness than the bank clerk had done. She seemed, indeed, to be in a considerably greater state of depression than he. Should anyone suppose that this was the effect of the verses themselves, it is only fair to say that the specimen verse of the Post Office Hymn ran thus:

> 'O'er London our letters are shaken like snow,
> Our wires o'er the world like the thunderbolts go.
> The news that may marry a maiden in Sark,
> Or kill an old lady in Finsbury Park.'

> Chorus (with a swing of joy and energy):

> 'Or kill an old lady in Finsbury Park.'

And the more I thought about the matter the more painfully certain it seemed that the most important and typical modern things could not be done with a chorus. One could not, for instance, be a great financier and sing; because the essence of being a great financier is that you keep quiet. You could not even in many modern circles be a public man and sing; because in those circles the essence of being a public man is that you do nearly everything in private. Nobody would imagine a chorus of money-lenders. Everyone knows the story of the solicitors' corps of volunteers who, when the Colonel on the battlefield cried 'Charge!' all said simultaneously, 'Six-and-eightpence.' Men can sing while charging in a military, but hardly in a legal sense. And at the end of my reflections I had really got no further than the subconscious feeling of my friend the bank clerk – that there is something spiritually suffocating about our life; not about our laws merely, but about our life. Bank clerks are without songs not because they are poor, but because they are sad. Sailors are much poorer. As I passed homewards I passed a little tin building of some religious sort, which was shaken with shouting as a trumpet is torn with its own tongue. *They* were singing anyhow; and I had for an instant a fancy I had often had before: that with us the super-human is the only place where you can find the human. Human nature is hunted, and has fled into sanctuary.

POEMS AT HOME

[Chesterton records one of many similar happenings involved with poetry in the company of Auberon Herbert, Maurice Baring, Hilaire Belloc and others, in his *Autobiography*.]

I once smashed an ordinary tumbler at Herbert's table, and an ever-blossoming tradition sprang up that it had been a vessel of inconceivable artistic and monetary value, its price perpetually mounting into millions and its form and colour taking on the glories of the Arabian Nights. From this incident (and from the joyful manner in which Baring trampled like an elephant among the fragments of the crystal) arose a catchword used by many of us in many subsequent controversies, in defence of romantic and revolutionary things; the expression: 'I like the noise of breaking glass.' I made it the refrain of a ballade which began:

> Prince, when I took your goblet tall
> And smashed it with inebriate care,
> I knew not how from Rome and Gaul
> You gained it; I was unaware
> It stood by Charlemagne's great chair
> And served St. Peter at High Mass.
> . . . I'm sorry if the thing was rare;
> I like the noise of breaking glass.

THE REVOLUTIONIST: OR LINES TO A STATESMAN

'I was never standing by while a revolution was going on.' –
Speech by the Rt. Hon. Walter Long.

[Published 18 December 1909 in the *Nation*.]

When Death was on thy drums, Democracy,
And with one rush of slaves the world was free,
In that high dawn that Kings shall not forget,
A void there was and Walter was not yet.
Through sacked Versailles, at Valmy in the fray,
They did without him in some kind of way;
Red Christendom all Walterless they cross,
And in their fury hardly feel their loss . . .

Fades the Republic; faint as Roland's horn,
Her trumpets taunt us with a sacred scorn . . .
Then silence fell: and Mr. Long was born.

From his first hours in his expensive cot
He never saw the tiniest viscount shot.
In deference to his wealthy parents' whim
The mildest massacres were kept from him.
The wars that dyed Pall Mall and Brompton red
Passed harmless o'er that one unconscious head:
For all that little Long could understand
The rich might still be rulers of the land,
Vain are the pious arts of parenthood,
Foiled Revolution bubbled in his blood;
Until one day (the babe unborn shall rue it)
The Constitution bored him and he slew it.

If I were wise and good and rich and strong –
Fond, impious thought, if I were Walter Long –
If I could water sell like molten gold,
And make grown people do as they were told,
If over private fields and wastes as wide
As a Greek city for which heroes died,
I owned the houses and the men inside –
If all this hung on one thin thread of habit
I would not revolutionize a rabbit.

I would sit tight with all my gifts and glories,
And even preach to unconverted Tories,
That the fixed system that our land inherits,
Viewed from a certain standpoint, has its merits.
I'd guard the laws like any Radical,
And keep each precedent, however small,
However subtle, misty, dusty, dreamy,
Lest man by chance should look at me and see me;
Lest men should ask what madman made me lord
Of English ploughshares and the English sword;
Lest men should mark how sleepy is the nod
That drills the dreadful images of God!

Walter, be wise! avoid the wild and new!
The Constitution is the game for you.
Walter, beware! scorn not the gathering throng,
It suffers, yet it may not suffer wrong,
It suffers, yet it cannot suffer Long.
And if you goad it these grey rules to break,
For a few pence, see that you do not wake
Death and the splendour of the scarlet cap,
Boston and Valmy, Yorktown and Jemmappes,
Freedom in arms, the riding and the routing,
The thunder of the captains and the shouting,
All that lost riot that you did not share –
And when that riot comes – you *will* be there.

(ii) THE BALLAD OF THE WHITE HORSE (1911)

[See Introduction. It should be added here that, although there is much legend, invention and inspiration in the poem, there is a great deal of history beyond the general story: e.g. in the first Book, Alfred's attraction as a child to an illuminated initial in a book shown him by his mother, and the Alfred Jewel found near Athelney; or in the last Book the little commonplace book which he always carried with him, and the voyages of Ohthere and Wulfstan to the North. The Dedication is to Frances Chesterton. The Latin text in Book VI verse 36 is the Vulgate version of Psalm 76 verse 3: 'he broke the powers of the bows, the shield, the sword, and the battle'.

The text of the version in *Collected Poems* (1927) was much improved, probably with the help of Dorothy Collins. But I have ventured to correct what seem two obvious misprints, 'small' for 'shall' in Book IV, verse 52 and 'this' for 'his' in Book VII, verse 68.]

DEDICATION

Of great limbs gone to chaos,
  A great face turned to night –
Why bend above a shapeless shroud
Seeking in such archaic cloud
  Sight of strong lords and light?

Where seven sunken Englands
  Lie buried one by one,
Why should one idle spade, I wonder,
Shake up the dust of thanes like thunder
  To smoke and choke the sun?

In cloud of clay so cast to heaven
  What shape shall man discern?
These lords may light the mystery
Of mastery or victory,
And these ride high in history,
  But these shall not return.

Gored on the Norman gonfalon
  The Golden Dragon died:
We shall not wake with ballad strings
The good time of the smaller things,
We shall not see the holy kings
  Ride down by Severn side.

[74]

Stiff, strange, and quaintly coloured
  As the broidery of Bayeux
The England of that dawn remains,
And this of Alfred and the Danes
Seems like the tales a whole tribe feigns
  Too English to be true.

Of a good king on an island
  That ruled once on a time;
And as he walked by an apple tree
There came green devils out of the sea
With sea-plants trailing heavily
  And tracks of opal slime.

Yet Alfred is no fairy tale;
  His days as our days ran,
He also looked forth for an hour
On peopled plains and skies that lower,
From those few windows in the tower
  That is the head of a man.

But who shall look from Alfred's hood
  Or breathe his breath alive?
His century like a small dark cloud
Drifts far; it is an eyeless crowd,
Where the tortured trumpets scream aloud
  And the dense arrows drive.

Lady, by one light only
  We look from Alfred's eyes,
We know he saw athwart the wreck
The sign that hangs about your neck,
Where One more than Melchizedek
  Is dead and never dies.

Therefore I bring these rhymes to you.
  Who brought the cross to me,
Since on you flaming without flaw
I saw the sign that Guthrum saw

When he let break his ships of awe,
  And laid peace on the sea.

Do you remember when we went
  Under a dragon moon,
And 'mid volcanic tints of night
Walked where they fought the unknown fight
And saw black trees on the battle-height,
  Black thorn on Ethandune?

And I thought, 'I will go with you,
  As man with God has gone,
And wander with a wandering star,
The wandering heart of things that are,
The fiery cross of love and war
  That like yourself, goes on.'

O go you onward; where you are
  Shall honour and laughter be,
Past purpled forest and pearled foam,
God's winged pavilion free to roam,
Your face, that is a wandering home,
  A flying home for me.

Ride through the silent earthquake lands,
  Wide as a waste is wide,
Across these days like deserts, when
Pride and a little scratching pen
Have dried and split the hearts of men,
  Heart of the heroes, ride.

Up through an empty house of stars,
  Being what heart you are,
Up the inhuman steeps of space
As on a staircase go in grace,
Carrying the firelight on your face
  Beyond the loneliest star.

Take these; in memory of the hour
    We strayed a space from home
And saw the smoke-hued hamlets, quaint
With Westland king and Westland saint,
And watched the western glory faint
    Along the road to Frome.

BOOK I

THE VISION OF THE KING

Before the gods that made the gods
    Had seen their sunrise pass,
The White Horse of the White Horse Vale
    Was cut out of the grass.

Before the gods that made the gods
    Had drunk at dawn their fill,
The White Horse of the White Horse Vale
    Was hoary on the hill.

Age beyond age on British land,
    Æons on æons gone,
Was peace and war in western hills,
    And the White Horse looked on.

For the White Horse knew England
    When there was none to know;
He saw the first oar break or bend,
He saw heaven fall and the world end,
    O God, how long ago.

For the end of the world was long ago –
    And all we dwell to-day
As children of some second birth,
Like a strange people left on earth
    After a judgment day.

For the end of the world was long ago,
   When the ends of the world waxed free,
When Rome was sunk in a waste of slaves,
   And the sun drowned in the sea.

When Cæsar's sun fell out of the sky
   And whoso hearkened right
Could only hear the plunging
   Of the nations in the night.

When the ends of the earth came marching in
   To torch and cresset gleam.
And the roads of the world that lead to Rome
Were filled with faces that moved like foam,
   Like faces in a dream.

And men rode out of the eastern lands,
   Broad river and burning plain;
Trees that are Titan flowers to see,
And tiger skies, striped horribly,
   With tints of tropic rain.

Where Ind's enamelled peaks arise
   Around that inmost one,
Where ancient eagles on its brink,
Vast as archangels, gather and drink
   The sacrament of the sun.

And men brake out of the northern lands,
   Enormous lands alone,
Where a spell is laid upon life and lust
And the rain is changed to a silver dust
   And the sea to a great green stone.

And a Shape that moveth murkily
   In mirrors of ice and night,
Hath blanched with fear all beasts and birds,
As death and a shock of evil words
   Blast a man's hair with white.

And the cry of the palms and the purple moons,
    Or the cry of the frost and foam,
Swept ever around an inmost place,
And the din of distant race on race
    Cried and replied round Rome.

And there was death on the Emperor
    And night upon the Pope:
And Alfred, hiding in deep grass,
    Hardened his heart with hope.

A sea-folk blinder than the sea
    Broke all about his land,
But Alfred up against them bare
And gripped the ground and grasped the air,
    Staggered, and strove to stand.

He bent them back with spear and spade,
    With desperate dyke and wall,
With foemen leaning on his shield
And roaring on him when he reeled;
    And no help came at all.

He broke them with a broken sword
    A little towards the sea,
And for one hour of panting peace,
Ringed with a roar that would not cease,
With golden crown and girded fleece
    Made laws under a tree.
        .   .   .   .   .

The Northmen came about our land
    A Christless chivalry:
Who knew not of the arch or pen,
Great, beautiful half-witted men
    From the sunrise and the sea.

Misshapen ships stood on the deep
    Full of strange gold and fire,
And hairy men, as huge as sin

With hornèd heads, came wading in
    Through the long, low sea-mire.

Our towns were shaken of tall kings
    With scarlet beards like blood:
The world turned empty where they trod,
They took the kindly cross of God
    And cut it up for wood.

Their souls were drifting as the sea,
    And all good towns and lands
They only saw with heavy eyes,
    And broke with heavy hands.

Their gods were sadder than the sea,
    Gods of a wandering will,
Who cried for blood like beasts at night,
    Sadly, from hill to hill.

They seemed as trees walking the earth,
    As witless and as tall,
Yet they took hold upon the heavens
    And no help came at all.

They bred like birds in English woods,
    They rooted like the rose,
When Alfred came to Athelney
    To hide him from their bows

There was not English armour left,
    Nor any English thing,
When Alfred came to Athelney
    To be an English king.

For earthquake swallowing earthquake
    Uprent the Wessex tree;
The whirlpool of the pagan sway
Had swirled his sires as sticks away
    When a flood smites the sea.

And the great kings of Wessex
    Wearied and sank in gore,
And even their ghosts in that great stress
Grew greyer and greyer, less and less,
With the lords that died in Lyonesse
    And the king that comes no more.

And the God of the Golden Dragon
    Was dumb upon his throne,
And the lord of the Golden Dragon
    Ran in the woods alone.

And if ever he climbed the crest of luck
    And set the flag before,
Returning as a wheel returns,
Came ruin and the rain that burns,
    And all began once more.

And naught was left King Alfred
    But shameful tears of rage,
In the island in the river
    In the end of all his age.

In the island in the river
    He was broken to his knee:
And he read, writ with an iron pen,
That God had wearied of Wessex men
And given their country, field and fen,
    To the devils of the sea.

And he saw in a little picture,
    Tiny and far away,
His mother sitting in Egbert's hall,
And a book she showed him, very small,
Where a sapphire Mary sat in stall
    With a golden Christ at play.

It was wrought in the monk's slow manner,
    From silver and sanguine shell,

Where the scenes are little and terrible,
  Keyholes of heaven and hell.

In the river island of Athelney,
  With the river running past,
In colours of such simple creed
All things sprang at him, sun and weed,
Till the grass grew to be grass indeed
  And the tree was a tree at last.

Fearfully plain the flowers grew,
  Like the child's book to read,
Or like a friend's face seen in a glass;
He looked; and there Our Lady was,
She stood and stroked the tall live grass
  As a man strokes his steed.

Her face was like an open word
  When brave men speak and choose,
The very colours of her coat
  Were better than good news.

She spoke not, nor turned not,
  Nor any sign she cast,
Only she stood up straight and free,
Between the flowers in Athelney,
  And the river running past.

One dim ancestral jewel hung
  On his ruined armour grey,
He rent and cast it at her feet:
Where, after centuries, with slow feet,
Men came from hall and school and street
  And found it where it lay.

'Mother of God, ' the wanderer said,
  'I am but a common king,
Nor will I ask what saints may ask,
  To see a secret thing.

'The gates of heaven are fearful gates
  Worse than the gates of hell;
Not I would break the splendours barred
Or seek to know the thing they guard,
  Which is too good to tell.

'But for this earth most pitiful,
  This little land I know,
If that which is for ever is,
Or if our hearts shall break with bliss,
  Seeing the stranger go?

'When our last bow is broken, Queen,
  And our last javelin cast,
Under some sad, green evening sky,
Holding a ruined cross on high,
Under warm westland grass to lie,
  Shall we come home at last?'

And a voice came human but high up,
  Like a cottage climbed among
The clouds; or a serf of hut and croft
That sits by his hovel fire as oft,
But hears on his old bare roof aloft
  A belfry burst in song.

'The gates of heaven are lightly locked,
  We do not guard our gain,
The heaviest hind may easily
Come silently and suddenly
  Upon me in a lane.

'And any little maid that walks
  In good thoughts apart,
May break the guard of the Three Kings
And see the dear and dreadful things
  I hid within my heart.

'The meanest man in grey fields gone
    Behind the set of sun,
Heareth between star and other star,
Through the door of the darkness fallen ajar,
The council, eldest of things that are,
    The talk of the Three in One.

'The gates of heaven are lightly locked,
    We do not guard our gold,
Men may uproot where worlds begin,
Or read the name of the nameless sin;
But if he fail or if he win
    To no good man is told.

'The men of the East may spell the stars,
    And times and triumphs mark,
But the men signed of the cross of Christ
    Go gaily in the dark.

'The men of the East may search the scrolls
    For sure fates and fame,
But the men that drink the blood of God
    Go singing to their shame.

'The wise men know what wicked things
    Are written on the sky,
They trim sad lamps, they touch sad strings,
Hearing the heavy purple wings,
Where the forgotten seraph kings
    Still plot how God shall die.

'The wise men know all evil things
    Under the twisted trees,
Where the perverse in pleasure pine
And men are weary of green wine
    And sick of crimson seas.

'But you and all the kind of Christ
    Are ignorant and brave,

And you have wars you hardly win
   And souls you hardly save.

'I tell you naught for your comfort,
   Yea, naught for your desire,
Save that the sky grows darker yet
   And the sea rises higher.

'Night shall be thrice night over you,
   And heaven an iron cope.
Do you have joy without a cause,
   Yea, faith without a hope?'

Even as she spoke she was not,
   Nor any word said he,
He only heard, still as he stood
Under the old night's nodding hood,
The sea-folk breaking down the wood
   Like a high tide from sea.

He only heard the heathen men,
   Whose eyes are blue and bleak,
Singing about some cruel thing
Done by a great and smiling king
   In daylight on a deck.

He only heard the heathen men,
   Whose eyes are blue and blind,
Singing what shameful things are done
Between the sunlit sea and the sun
   When the land is left behind.

BOOK II

THE GATHERING OF THE CHIEFS

Up across windy wastes and up
   Went Alfred over the shaws,

Shaken of the joy of giants,
   The joy without a cause.

In the slopes away to the western bays,
   Where blows not ever a tree,
He washed his soul in the west wind
   And his body in the sea.

And he set to rhyme his ale-measures,
   And he sang aloud his laws,
Because of the joy of the giants,
   The joy without a cause.

For the King went gathering Wessex men,
   As grain out of the chaff
The few that were alive to die,
Laughing, as littered skulls that lie
After lost battles turn to the sky
   An everlasting laugh.

The King went gathering Christian men,
   As wheat out of the husk;
Eldred, the Franklin by the sea,
And Mark, the man from Italy,
And Colan of the Sacred Tree,
   From the old tribe on Usk.

The rook croaked homeward heavily,
   The west was clear and warm,
The smoke of evening food and ease
Rose like a blue tree in the trees
   When he came to Eldred's farm.

But Eldred's farm was fallen awry,
   Like an old cripple's bones,
And Eldred's tools were red with rust,
And on his well was a green crust,
And purple thistles upward thrust,
   Between the kitchen stones.

But smoke of some good feasting
  Went upwards evermore,
And Eldred's doors stood wide apart
For loitering foot or labouring cart,
And Eldred's great and foolish heart
  Stood open like his door.

A mighty man was Eldred,
  A bulk for casks to fill,
His face a dreaming furnace,
  His body a walking hill.

In the old wars of Wessex
  His sword had sunken deep,
But all his friends, he sighed and said,
Were broken about Ethelred;
And between the deep drink and the dead
  He had fallen upon sleep.

'Come not to me, King Alfred,
  Save always for the ale:
Why should my harmless hinds be slain
Because the chiefs cry once again,
As in all fights, that we shall gain,
  And in all fights we fail?

'Your scalds still thunder and prophesy
  That crown that never comes;
Friend, I will watch the certain things,
Swine, and slow moons like silver rings,
  And the ripening of the plums.'

And Alfred answered, drinking,
  And gravely, without blame,
'Nor bear I boast of scald or king,
The thing I bear is a lesser thing,
  But comes in a better name.

'Out of the mouth of the Mother of God,
  More than the doors of doom,
I call the muster of Wessex men
From grassy hamlet or ditch or den,
To break and be broken, God knows when,
  But I have seen for whom.

'Out of the mouth of the Mother of God
  Like a little word come I;
For I go gathering Christian men
From sunken paving and ford and fen,
To die in a battle, God knows when,
  By God, but I know why.

'And this is the word of Mary,
  The word of the world's desire:
"No more of comfort shall ye get,
Save that the sky grows darker yet
  And the sea rises higher." '

Then silence sank. And slowly
  Arose the sea-land lord,
Like some vast beast for mystery,
He filled the room and porch and sky,
And from a cobwebbed nail on high
  Unhooked his heavy sword.

Up on the shrill sea-downs and up
  Went Alfred all alone,
Turning but once e'er the door was shut,
Shouting to Eldred over his butt,
That he bring all spears to the woodman's hut
  Hewn under Egbert's Stone.

And he turned his back and broke the fern,
  And fought the moths of dusk,
And went on his way for other friends,
Friends fallen of all the wide world's ends,

From Rome that wrath and pardon sends
  And the grey tribes on Usk.

He saw gigantic tracks of death
  And many a shape of doom,
Good steadings to grey ashes gone
And a monk's house white like a skeleton
  In the green crypt of the combe.

And in many a Roman villa
  Earth and her ivies eat,
Saw coloured pavements sink and fade
In flowers, and the windy colonnade
  Like the spectre of a street.

But the cold stars clustered
  Among the cold pines
Ere he was half on his pilgrimage
  Over the western lines.

And the white dawn widened
  Ere he came to the last pine,
Where Mark, the man from Italy,
  Still made the Christian sign.

The long farm lay on the large hill-side,
  Flat like a painted plan,
And by the side the low white house,
  Where dwelt the southland man.

A bronzed man, with a bird's bright eye,
  And a strong bird's beak and brow,
His skin was brown like buried gold,
And of certain of his sires was told
That they came in the shining ship of old,
  With Caesar in the prow.

His fruit trees stood like soldiers
  Drilled in a straight line,

His strange, stiff olives did not fail,
And all the kings of the earth drank ale,
　　But he drank wine.

Wide over wasted British plains
　　Stood never an arch or dome,
Only the trees to toss and reel,
The tribes to bicker, the beasts to squeal;
But the eyes in his head were strong like steel,
　　And his soul remembered Rome.

Then Alfred of the lonely spear
　　Lifted his lion head;
And fronted with the Italian's eye,
Asking him of his whence and why,
　　King Alfred stood and said:

'I am that oft-defeated King
　　Whose failure fills the land,
Who fled before the Danes of old,
Who chaffered with the Danes with gold,
Who now upon the Wessex wold
　　Hardly has feet to stand.

'But out of the mouth of the Mother of God
　　I have seen the truth like fire,
This – that the sky grows darker yet
　　And the sea rises higher.'

Long looked the Roman on the land;
　　The trees as golden crowns
Blazed, drenched with dawn and dew-empearled
While faintlier coloured, freshlier curled,
The clouds from underneath the world
　　Stood up over the downs.

'These vines be ropes that drag me hard, '
　　He said. 'I go not far;
Where would you meet? For you must hold

Half Wiltshire and the White Horse wold,
And the Thames bank to Owsenfold,
   If Wessex goes to war.

'Guthrum sits strong on either bank
   And you must press his lines
Inwards, and eastward drive him down;
I doubt if you shall take the crown
Till you have taken London town.
   For me, I have the vines.'

'If each man on the Judgment Day
   Meet God on a plain alone, '
Said Alfred, 'I will speak for you
As for myself, and call it true
That you brought all fighting folk you knew
   Lined under Egbert's Stone.

'Though I be in the dust ere then,
   I know where you will be.'
And shouldering suddenly his spear
He faded like some elfin fear,
Where the tall pines ran up, tier on tier,
   Tree overtoppling tree.

He shouldered his spear at morning
   And laughed to lay it on,
But he leaned on his spear as on a staff,
With might and little mood to laugh,
Or ever he sighted chick or calf
   Of Colan of Caerleon.

For the man dwelt in a lost land
   Of boulders and broken men,
In a great grey cave far off to the south
Where a thick green forest stopped the mouth,
   Giving darkness in his den.

And the man was come like a shadow,
  From the shadow of Druid trees,
Where Usk, with mighty murmurings,
Past Caerleon of the fallen kings,
  Goes out to ghostly seas.

Last of a race in ruin –
  He spoke the speech of the Gaels;
His kin were in holy Ireland,
  Or up in the crags of Wales.

But his soul stood with his mother's folk,
  That were of the rain-wrapped isle,
Where Patrick and Brandan westerly
Looked out at last on a landless sea
  And the sun's last smile.

His harp was carved and cunning,
  As the Celtic craftsman makes,
Graven all over with twisting shapes
  Like many headless snakes.

His harp was carved and cunning,
  His sword prompt and sharp,
And he was gay when he held the sword,
  Sad when he held the harp.

For the great Gaels of Ireland
  Are the men that God made mad,
For all their wars are merry,
  And all their songs are sad.

He kept the Roman order,
  He made the Christian sign;
But his eyes grew often blind and bright,
And the sea that rose in the rocks at night
  Rose to his head like wine.

He made the sign of the cross of God,
  He knew the Roman prayer,
But he had unreason in his heart
  Because of the gods that were.

Even they that walked on the high cliffs,
  High as the clouds were then,
Gods of unbearable beauty,
  That broke the hearts of men.

And whether in seat or saddle,
  Whether with frown or smile,
Whether at feast or fight was he,
He heard the noise of a nameless sea
  On an undiscovered isle.

Lifting the great green ivy
  And the great spear lowering,
One said, 'I am Alfred of Wessex,
  And I am a conquered king.'

And the man of the cave made answer,
  And his eyes were stars of scorn,
'And better kings were conquered
  Or ever your sires were born.

'What goddess was your mother,
  What fay your breed begot,
That you should not die with Uther
  And Arthur and Lancelot?

'But when you win you brag and blow,
  And when you lose you rail,
Army of eastland yokels
  Not strong enough to fail.'

'I bring not boast or railing,'
  Spake Alfred not in ire,
'I bring of Our Lady a lesson set,

This – that the sky grows darker yet
   And the sea rises higher.'

Then Colan of the Sacred Tree
   Tossed his black mane on high,
And cried, as rigidly he rose,
'And if the sea and sky be foes,
   We will tame the sea and sky.'

Smiled Alfred, 'Seek ye a fable
   More dizzy and more dread
Than all your mad barbarian tales
   Where the sky stands on its head?

'A tale where a man looks down on the sky
   That has long looked down on him;
A tale where a man can swallow a sea
   That might swallow the seraphim.

'Bring to the hut by Egbert's Stone
   All bills and bows ye have.'
And Alfred strode off rapidly,
And Colan of the Sacred Tree
   Went slowly to his cave.

BOOK III

THE HARP OF ALFRED

In a tree that yawned and twisted
   The King's few goods were flung,
A mass-book mildewed, line by line,
And weapons and a skin of wine,
   And an old harp unstrung.

By the yawning tree in the twilight
   The King unbound his sword,
Severed the harp of all his goods,

And there in the cool and soundless woods
  Sounded a single chord.

Then laughed; and watched the finches flash,
  The sullen flies in swarm,
And went unarmed over the hills,
  With the harp upon his arm,

Until he came to the White Horse Vale
  And saw across the plains,
In the twilight high and far and fell,
Like the fiery terraces of hell,
  The camp fires of the Danes –

The fires of the Great Army
  That was made of iron men,
Whose lights of sacrilege and scorn
Ran around England red as morn,
Fires over Glastonbury Thorn –
  Fires out on Ely Fen.

And as he went by White Horse Vale
  He saw lie wan and wide
The old horse graven, God knows when,
By gods or beasts or what things then
Walked a new world instead of men
  And scrawled on the hill-side.

And when he came to White Horse Down
  The great White Horse was grey,
For it was ill scoured of the weed,
And lichen and thorn could crawl and feed,
Since the foes of settled house and creed
  Had swept old works away.

King Alfred gazed all sorrowful
  At thistle and mosses grey,
Till a rally of Danes with shield and bill
Rolled drunk over the dome of the hill,

And, hearing of his harp and skill,
  They dragged him to their play.

And as they went through the high green grass
  They roared like the great green sea;
But when they came to the red camp fire
  They were silent suddenly.

And as they went up the wastes away
  They went reeling to and fro;
But when they came to the red camp fire
  They stood all in a row.

For golden in the firelight,
  With a smile carved on his lips,
And a beard curled right cunningly,
Was Guthrum of the Northern Sea,
  The emperor of the ships –

With three great earls King Guthrum
  Went the rounds from fire to fire,
With Harold, nephew of the King,
And Ogier of the Stone and Sling,
And Elf, whose gold lute had a string
  That sighed like all desire.

The Earls of the Great Army
  That no men born could tire,
Whose flames anear him or aloof
Took hold of towers or walls of proof,
Fire over Glastonbury roof
  And out on Ely, fire.

And Guthrum heard the soldiers' tale
  And bade the stranger play;
Not harshly, but as one on high,
On a marble pillar in the sky,
Who sees all folk that live and die –
  Pigmy and far away.

And Alfred, King of Wessex,
  Looked on his conqueror –
And his hands hardened; but he played,
And leaving all later hates unsaid,
He sang of some old British raid
  On the wild west march of yore.

He sang of war in the warm wet shires,
  Where rain nor fruitage fails,
Where England of the motley states
Deepens like a garden to the gates
  In the purple walls of Wales.

He sang of the seas of savage heads
  And the seas and seas of spears,
Boiling all over Offa's Dyke,
What time a Wessex club could strike
  The kings of the mountaineers.

Till Harold laughed and snatched the harp,
  The kinsman of the King,
A big youth, beardless like a child,
Whom the new wine of war sent wild,
  Smote, and began to sing –

And he cried of the ships as eagles
  That circle fiercely and fly,
And sweep the seas and strike the towns
  From Cyprus round to Skye.

How swiftly and with peril
  They gather all good things,
The high horns of the forest beasts,
  Or the secret stones of kings.

'For Rome was given to rule the world,
  And gat of it little joy –
But we, but we shall enjoy the world,
  The whole huge world a toy.

[97]

'Great wine like blood from Burgundy,
  Cloaks like the clouds from Tyre,
And marble like solid moonlight,
  And gold like frozen fire.

'Smells that a man might swill in a cup,
  Stones that a man might eat,
And the great smooth women like ivory
  That the Turks sell in the street.'

He sang the song of the thief of the world,
  And the gods that love the thief;
And he yelled aloud at the cloister-yards,
  Where men go gathering grief.

'Well have you sung, O stranger,
  Of death on the dyke in Wales,
Your chief was a bracelet-giver;
But the red unbroken river
Of a race runs not for ever,
  But suddenly it fails.

'Doubtless your sires were sword-swingers
  When they waded fresh from foam,
Before they were turned to women
  By the god of the nails from Rome;

'But since you bent to the shaven men,
  Who neither lust nor smite,
Thunder of Thor, we hunt you
  A hare on the mountain height.'

King Guthrum smiled a little,
  And said, 'It is enough,
Nephew, let Elf retune the string;
A boy must needs like bellowing,
But the old ears of a careful king
  Are glad of songs less rough.'

Blue-eyed was Elf the minstrel,
  With womanish hair and ring,
Yet heavy was his hand on sword,
  Though light upon the string.

And as he stirred the strings of the harp
  To notes but four or five,
The heart of each man moved in him
  Like a babe buried alive.

And they felt the land of the folk-songs
  Spread southward of the Dane,
And they heard the good Rhine flowing
  In the heart of all Allemagne.

They felt the land of the folk-songs,
  Where the gifts hang on the tree,
Where the girls give ale at morning
  And the tears come easily.

The mighty people, womanlike,
  That have pleasure in their pain
As he sang of Balder beautiful,
  Whom the heavens loved in vain.

As he sang of Balder beautiful,
  Whom the heavens could not save,
Till the world was like a sea of tears
  And every soul a wave.

'There is always a thing forgotten
  When all the world goes well;
A thing forgotten, as long ago,
When the gods forgot the mistletoe,
And soundless as an arrow of snow
  The arrow of anguish fell.

'The thing on the blind side of the heart,
  On the wrong side of the door,

The green plant groweth, menacing
Almighty lovers in the spring;
There is always a forgotten thing,
   And love is not secure.'

And all that sat by the fire were sad,
   Save Ogier, who was stern,
And his eyes hardened, even to stones,
   As he took the harp in turn;

Earl Ogier of the Stone and Sling
   Was odd to ear and sight,
Old he was, but his locks were red,
And jests were all the words he said,
Yet he was sad at board and bed
   And savage in the fight.

'You sing of the young gods easily
   In the days when you are young;
But I go smelling yew and sods,
And I know there are gods behind the gods,
   Gods that are best unsung.

'And a man grows ugly for women,
   And a man grows dull with ale,
Well if he find in his soul at last
   Fury, that does not fail.

'The wrath of the gods behind the gods
   Who would rend all gods and men,
Well if the old man's heart hath still
Wheels sped of rage and roaring will,
Like cataracts to break down and kill,
   Well for the old man then –

'While there is one tall shrine to shake,
   Or one live man to rend;
For the wrath of the gods behind the gods
   Who are weary to make an end.

'There lives one moment for a man
   When the door at his shoulder shakes,
When the taut rope parts under the pull,
And the barest branch is beautiful
   One moment, while it breaks.

'So rides my soul upon the sea
   That drinks the howling ships,
Though in black jest it bows and nods
Under the moons with silver rods,
I know it is roaring at the gods,
   Waiting the last eclipse.

'And in the last eclipse the sea
   Shall stand up like a tower,
Above all moons made dark and riven,
Hold up its foaming head in heaven,
   And laugh, knowing its hour.

'And the high ones in the happy town
   Propped of the planets seven,
Shall know a new light in the mind,
A noise about them and behind,
Shall hear an awful voice, and find
   Foam in the courts of heaven.

'And you that sit by the fire are young,
   And true love waits for you;
But the king and I grow old, grow old,
   And hate alone is true.'

And Guthrum shook his head but smiled,
   For he was a mighty clerk,
And had read lines in the Latin books
   When all the north was dark.

He said, 'I am older than you, Ogier;
   Not all things would I rend,
For whether life be bad or good
   It is best to abide the end.'

He took the great harp wearily,
  Even Guthrum of the Danes,
With wide eyes bright as the one long day
  On the long polar plains.

For he sang of a wheel returning,
  And the mire trod back to mire,
And how red hells and golden heavens
  Are castles in the fire.

'It is good to sit where the good tales go,
  To sit as our fathers sat;
But the hour shall come after his youth,
When a man shall know not tales but truth,
  And his heart fail thereat.

'When he shall read what is written
  So plain in clouds and clods,
When he shall hunger without hope
  Even for evil gods.

'For this is a heavy matter,
  And the truth is cold to tell;
Do we not know, have we not heard,
The soul is like a lost bird,
  The body a broken shell.

'And a man hopes, being ignorant,
  Till in white woods apart
He finds at last the lost bird dead:
And a man may still lift up his head
  But never more his heart.

'There comes no noise but weeping
  Out of the ancient sky,
And a tear is in the tiniest flower
  Because the gods must die.

'The little brooks are very sweet,
    Like a girl's ribbons curled,
But the great sea is bitter
    That washes all the world.

'Strong are the Roman roses,
    Or the free flowers of the heath,
But every flower, like a flower of the sea,
    Smelleth with the salt of death.

'And the heart of the locked battle
    Is the happiest place for men;
When shrieking souls as shafts go by
And many have died and all may die;
Though this word be a mystery,
    Death is most distant then.

'Death blazes bright above the cup,
    And clear above the crown;
But in that dream of battle
    We seem to tread it down.

'Wherefore I am a great king,
    And waste the world in vain,
Because man hath not other power,
Save that in dealing death for dower,
He may forget it for an hour
    To remember it again.'

And slowly his hands and thoughtfully
    Fell from the lifted lyre,
And the owls moaned from the mighty trees
Till Alfred caught it to his knees
    And smote it as in ire.

He heaved the head of the harp on high
    And swept the framework barred,
And his stroke had all the rattle and spark
    Of horses flying hard.

[103]

'When God put man in a garden
  He girt him with a sword,
And sent him forth a free knight
  That might betray his lord;

'He brake Him and betrayed Him,
  And fast and far he fell,
Till you and I may stretch our necks
  And burn our beards in hell.

'But though I lie on the floor of the world,
  With the seven sins for rods,
I would rather fall with Adam
  Than rise with all your gods.

'What have the strong gods given?
  Where have the glad gods led?
When Guthrum sits on a hero's throne
  And asks if he is dead?

'Sirs, I am but a nameless man,
  A rhymester without home,
Yet since I come of the Wessex clay
  And carry the cross of Rome,

'I will even answer the mighty earl
  That asked of Wessex men
Why they be meek and monkish folk,
And bow to the White Lord's broken yoke;
What sign have we save blood and smoke?
  Here is my answer then.

'That on you is fallen the shadow,
  And not upon the Name;
That though we scatter and though we fly,
And you hang over us like the sky,
You are more tired of victory,
  Than we are tired of shame.

'That though you hunt the Christian man
    Like a hare on the hill-side,
The hare has still more heart to run
    Than you have heart to ride.

'That though all lances split on you,
    All swords be heaved in vain,
We have more lust again to lose
    Than you to win again.

'Your lord sits high in the saddle,
    A broken-hearted king,
But our king Alfred, lost from fame,
Fallen among foes or bonds of shame,
In I know not what mean trade or name,
    Has still some song to sing;

'Our monks go robed in rain and snow,
    But the heart of flame therein,
But you go clothed in feasts and flames,
    When all is ice within;

'Nor shall all iron dooms make dumb
    Men wondering ceaselessly,
If it be not better to fast for joy
    Than feast for misery.

'Nor monkish order only
    Slides down, as field to fen,
All things achieved and chosen pass,
As the White Horse fades in the grass,
    No work of Christian men.

'Ere the sad gods that made your gods
    Saw their sad sunrise pass,
The White Horse of the White Horse Vale,
That you have left to darken and fail,
    Was cut out of the grass.

[105]

'Therefore your end is on you,
    Is on you and your kings,
Not for a fire in Ely fen,
Not that your gods are nine or ten,
But because it is only Christian men
    Guard even heathen things.

'For our God hath blessed creation,
    Calling it good. I know
What spirit with whom you blindly band
Hath blessed destruction with his hand;
Yet by God's death the stars shall stand
    And the small apples grow.'

And the King, with harp on shoulder,
    Stood up and ceased his song;
And the owls moaned from the mighty trees,
    And the Danes laughed loud and long.

BOOK IV

THE WOMAN IN THE FOREST

Thick thunder of the snorting swine,
    Enormous in the gloam,
Rending among all roots that cling,
And the wild horses whinnying,
Were the night's noises when the King
    Shouldering his harp, went home.

With eyes of owl and feet of fox,
    Full of all thoughts he went;
He marked the tilt of the pagan camp,
The paling of pine, the sentries' tramp,
And the one great stolen altar-lamp
    Over Guthrum in his tent.

By scrub and thorn in Ethandune
    That night the foe had lain;
Whence ran across the heather grey
The old stones of a Roman way;
And in a wood not far away
    The pale road split in twain.

He marked the wood and the cloven ways
    With an old captain's eyes,
And he thought how many a time had he
Sought to see Doom he could not see;
How ruin had come and victory,
    And both were a surprise.

Even so he had watched and wondered
    Under Ashdown from the plains;
With Ethelred praying in his tent,
Till the white hawthorn swung and bent,
As Alfred rushed his spears and rent
    The shield-wall of the Danes.

Even so he had watched and wondered,
    Knowing neither less nor more,
Till all his lords lay dying,
And axes on axes plying,
Flung him, and drove him flying
    Like a pirate to the shore.

Wise he had been before defeat,
    And wise before success;
Wise in both hours and ignorant,
    Knowing neither more nor less.

As he went down to the river-hut
    He knew a night-shade scent,
Owls did as evil cherubs rise,
With little wings and lantern eyes,
As though he sank through the under-skies;
    But down and down he went.

As he went down to the river-hut
  He went as one that fell;
Seeing the high forest domes and spars,
Dim green or torn with golden scars,
As the proud look up at the evil stars,
  In the red heavens of hell.

For he must meet by the river-hut
  Them he had bidden to arm,
Mark from the towers of Italy,
And Colan of the Sacred Tree,
And Eldred who beside the sea
  Held heavily his farm.

The roof leaned gaping to the grass,
  As a monstrous mushroom lies;
Echoing and empty seemed the place;
But opened in a little space
A great grey woman with scarred face
  And strong and humbled eyes.

King Alfred was but a meagre man,
  Bright eyed, but lean and pale:
And swordless, with his harp and rags,
He seemed a beggar, such as lags
  Looking for crusts and ale.

And the woman, with a woman's eyes
  Of pity at once and ire,
Said, when that she had glared a span,
'There is a cake for any man
  If he will watch the fire.'

And Alfred, bowing heavily,
  Sat down the fire to stir,
And even as the woman pitied him
  So did he pity her.

Saying, 'O great heart in the night,
    O best cast forth for worst,
Twilight shall melt and morning stir,
And no kind thing shall come to her,
Till God shall turn the world over
    And all the last are first.

'And well may God with the serving-folk
    Cast in His dreadful lot;
Is not He too a servant,
    And is not He forgot?

'For was not God my gardener
    And silent like a slave;
That opened oaks on the uplands
    Or thicket in graveyard gave?

'And was not God my armourer,
    All patient and unpaid,
That sealed my skull as a helmet,
    And ribs for hauberk made?

'Did not a great grey servant
    Of all my sires and me,
Build this pavilion of the pines,
    And herd the fowls and fill the vines,
And labour and pass and leave no signs
    Save mercy and mystery?

'For God is a great servant,
    And rose before the day,
From some primordial slumber torn;
But all we living later born
Sleep on, and rise after the morn
    And the Lord has gone away.

'On things half sprung from sleeping,
    All sleepy suns have shone,
They stretch stiff arms, the yawning trees,

The beasts blink upon hands and knees,
Man is awake and does and sees –
  But Heaven has done and gone.

'For who shall guess the good riddle
    Or speak of the Holiest,
Save in faint figures and failing words,
Who loves, yet laughs among the swords,
    Labours, and is at rest?

'But some see God like Guthrum,
    Crowned, with a great beard curled,
But I see God like a good giant,
    That, labouring, lifts the world.

'Wherefore was God in Golgotha,
    Slain as a serf is slain;
And hate He had of prince and peer,
And love He had and made good cheer,
Of them that, like this woman here,
    Go powerfully in pain.

'But in this grey morn of man's life,
    Cometh sometime to the mind
A little light that leaps and flies,
    Like a star blown on the wind.

'A star of nowhere, a nameless star,
    A light that spins and swirls,
And cries that even in hedge and hill,
Even on earth, it may go ill
    At last with the evil earls.

'A dancing sparkle, a doubtful star,
    On the waste wind whirled and driven;
But it seems to sing of a wilder worth,
A time discrowned of doom and birth,
And the kingdom of the poor on earth
    Come, as it is in heaven.

'But even though such days endure,
    How shall it profit her?
Who shall go groaning to the grave,
With many a meek and mighty slave,
Field-breaker and fisher on the wave,
    And woodman and waggoner.

'Bake ye the big world all again
    A cake with kinder leaven;
Yet these are sorry evermore–
Unless there be a little door,
    A little door in heaven.'

And as he wept for the woman
    He let her business be,
And like his royal oath and rash
The good food fell upon the ash
    And blackened instantly.

Screaming, the woman caught a cake
    Yet burning from the bar,
And struck him suddenly on the face,
    Leaving a scarlet scar.

King Alfred stood up wordless,
    A man dead with surprise,
And torture stood and the evil things
That are in the childish hearts of kings
    An instant in his eyes.

And even as he stood and stared
    Drew round him in the dusk
Those friends creeping from far-off farms,
Marcus with all his slaves in arms,
And the strange spears hung with ancient charms
    Of Colan of the Usk.

With one whole farm marching afoot
    The trampled road resounds,

Farm-hands and farm-beasts blundering by
And jars of mead and stores of rye,
Where Eldred strode above his high
   And thunder-throated hounds.

And grey cattle and silver lowed
   Against the unlifted morn,
And straw clung to the spear-shafts tall.
And a boy went before them all
   Blowing a ram's horn.

As mocking such rude revelry,
   The dim clan of the Gael
Came like a bad king's burial-end,
With dismal robes that drop and rend
   And demon pipes that wail–

In long, outlandish garments,
   Torn, though of antique worth,
With Druid beards and Druid spears,
As a resurrected race appears
   Out of an elder earth.

And though the King had called them forth
   And knew them for his own,
So still each eye stood like a gem,
So spectral hung each broidered hem,
Grey carven men he fancied them,
   Hewn in an age of stone.

And the two wild peoples of the north
   Stood fronting in the gloam,
And heard and knew each in its mind
The third great thunder on the wind,
The living walls that hedge mankind,
   The walking walls of Rome.

Mark's were the mixed tribes of the west,
   Of many a hue and strain,

Gurth, with rank hair like yellow grass,
And the Cornish fisher, Gorlias,
And Halmer, come from his first mass,
  Lately baptized, a Dane.

But like one man in armour
  Those hundreds trod the field,
From red Arabia to the Tyne
The earth had heard that marching-line,
Since the cry on the hill Capitoline,
  And the fall of the golden shield.

And the earth shook and the King stood still
  Under the greenwood bough,
And the smoking cake lay at his feet
  And the blow was on his brow.

Then Alfred laughed out suddenly
  Like thunder in the spring,
Till shook aloud the lintel-beams,
And the squirrels stirred in dusty dreams,
And the startled birds went up in streams,
  For the laughter of the King.

And the beasts of the earth and the birds looked down,
  In a wild solemnity,
On a stranger sight than a sylph or elf,
On one man laughing at himself
  Under the greenwood tree –

The giant laughter of Christian men
  That roars through a thousand tales,
Where greed is an ape and pride is an ass,
And Jack's away with his master's lass,
And the miser is banged with all his brass,
  The farmer with all his flails;

Tales that tumble and tales that trick,
  Yet end not all in scorning –

Of kings and clowns in a merry plight,
And the clock gone wrong and the world gone right,
That the mummers sing upon Christmas night
  And Christmas Day in the morning.

'Now here is a good warrant,'
  Cried Alfred, 'by my sword;
For he that is struck for an ill servant
  Should be a kind lord.

'He that has been a servant
  Knows more than priests and kings,
But he that has been an ill servant,
  He knows all earthly things.

'Pride flings frail palaces at the sky,
  As a man flings up sand,
But the firm feet of humility
  Take hold of heavy land.

'Pride juggles with her toppling towers,
  They strike the sun and cease,
But the firm feet of humility
  They grip the ground like trees.

'He that hath failed in a little thing
  Hath a sign upon the brow;
And the Earls of the Great Army
  Have no such seal to show.

'The red print on my forehead,
  Shall flame for a red star,
In the van of the violent marching, then
When the sky is torn of the trumpets ten,
And the hands of the happy howling men
  Fling wide the gates of war.

'This blow that I return not
  Ten times will I return
On kings and earls of all degree,
And armies wide as empires be

Shall slide like landslips to the sea
   If the red star burn.

'One man shall drive a hundred,
   As the dead kings drave;
Before me rocking hosts be riven,
And battering cohorts backwards driven,
For I am the first king known of Heaven
   That has been struck like a slave.

'Up on the old white road, brothers,
   Up on the Roman walls!
For this is the night of the drawing of swords,
And the tainted tower of the heathen hordes
Leans to our hammers, fires and cords,
   Leans a little and falls.

'Follow the star that lives and leaps,
   Follow the sword that sings,
For we go gathering heathen men,
A terrible harvest, ten by ten,
As the wrath of the last red autumn – then
   When Christ reaps down the kings.

'Follow a light that leaps and spins,
   Follow the fire unfurled!
For riseth up against realm and rod,
A thing forgotten, a thing downtrod,
The last lost giant, even God,
   Is risen against the world.'

Roaring they went o'er the Roman wall,
   And roaring up the lane,
Their torches tossed, a ladder of fire,
Higher their hymn was heard and higher,
More sweet for hate and for heart's desire,
And up in the northern scrub and brier,
   They fell upon the Dane.

BOOK V

ETHANDUNE: THE FIRST STROKE

King Guthrum was a dread king,
  Like death out of the north;
Shrines without name or number
He rent and rolled as lumber,
From Chester to the Humber
  He drove his foemen forth.

The Roman villas heard him
  In the valley of the Thames,
Come over the hills roaring
Above their roofs, and pouring
On spire and stair and flooring
  Brimstone and pitch and flames.

Sheer o'er the great chalk uplands
  And the hill of the Horse went he,
Till high on Hampshire beacons
  He saw the southern sea.

High on the heights of Wessex
  He saw the southern brine,
And turned him to a conquered land,
And where the northern thornwoods stand,
And the road parts on either hand,
  There came to him a sign.

King Guthrum was a war-chief,
  A wise man in the field,
And though he prospered well, and knew
How Alfred's folk were sad and few,
Not less with weighty care he drew
  Long lines for pike and shield.

King Guthrum lay on the upper land,
  On a single road at gaze,

And his foe must come with lean array,
Up the left arm of the cloven way,
　To the meeting of the ways.

And long ere the noise of armour,
　An hour ere the break of light,
The woods awoke with crash and cry,
And the birds sprang clamouring harsh and high,
And the rabbits ran like an elves' army
　Ere Alfred came in sight.

The live wood came at Guthrum,
　On foot and claw and wing,
The nests were noisy overhead,
For Alfred and the star of red,
All life went forth, and the forest fled
　Before the face of the King.

But halted in the woodways
　Christ's few were grim and grey,
And each with a small, far, bird-like sight
Saw the high folly of the fight;
And though strange joys had grown in the night,
　Despair grew with the day.

And when white dawn crawled through the wood,
　Like cold foam of a flood,
Then weakened every warrior's mood,
In hope, though not in hardihood;
And each man sorrowed as he stood
　In the fashion of his blood.

For the Saxon Franklin sorrowed
　For the things that had been fair;
For the dear dead woman, crimson-clad,
And the great feasts and the friends he had;
But the Celtic prince's soul was sad
　For the things that never were.

[117]

In the eyes Italian all things
  But a black laughter died;
And Alfred flung his shield to earth
  And smote his breast and cried –

'I wronged a man to his slaying,
  And a woman to her shame,
And once I looked on a sworn maid
  That was wed to the Holy Name.

'And once I took my neighbour's wife,
  That was bound to an eastland man,
In the starkness of my evil youth,
  Before my griefs began.

'People, if you have any prayers,
  Say prayers for me:
And lay me under a Christian stone
In that lost land I thought my own,
To wait till the holy horn is blown,
  And all poor men are free.'

Then Eldred of the idle farm
  Leaned on his ancient sword,
As fell his heavy words and few;
And his eyes were of such alien blue
As gleams where the Northman saileth new
  Into an unknown fiord.

'I was a fool and wasted ale –
  My slaves found it sweet;
I was a fool and wasted bread,
  And the birds had bread to eat.

'The kings go up and the kings go down,
  And who knows who shall rule;
Next night a king may starve or sleep,
But men and birds and beasts shall weep
  At the burial of a fool.

'O, drunkards in my cellar,
  Boys in my apple tree,
The world grows stern and strange and new,
And wise men shall govern you,
  And you shall weep for me.

'But yoke me my own oxen,
  Down to my own farm;
My own dog will whine for me,
My own friends will bend the knee,
And the foes I slew openly
  Have never wished me harm.'

And all were moved a little,
  But Colan stood apart,
Having first pity, and after
Hearing, like rat in rafter,
That little worm of laughter
  That eats the Irish heart.

And his grey-green eyes were cruel,
  And the smile of his mouth waxed hard,
And he said, 'And when did Britain
  Become your burying-yard?

'Before the Romans lit the land,
  When schools and monks were none,
We reared such stones to the sun-god
  As might put out the sun.

'The tall trees of Britain
  We worshipped and were wise,
But you shall raid the whole land through
And never a tree shall talk to you,
Though every leaf is a tongue taught true
  And the forest is full of eyes.

'On one round hill to the seaward
  The trees grow tall and grey

And the trees talk together
    When all men are away.

'O'er a few round hills forgotten
    The trees grow tall in rings,
And the trees talk together
    Of many pagan things.

'Yet I could lie and listen
    With a cross upon my clay,
And hear unhurt for ever
    What the trees of Britain say.'

A proud man was the Roman,
    His speech a single one,
But his eyes were like an eagle's eyes
    That is staring at the sun.

'Dig for me where I die,' he said,
    'If first or last I fall –
Dead on the fell at the first charge,
    Or dead by Wantage wall;

'Lift not my head from bloody ground,
    Bear not my body home,
For all the earth is Roman earth
    And I shall die in Rome.'

Then Alfred, King of England,
    Bade blow the horns of war,
And fling the Golden Dragon out,
With crackle and acclaim and shout,
    Scrolled and aflame and far.

And under the Golden Dragon
    Went Wessex all along,
Past the sharp point of the cloven ways,
Out from the black wood into the blaze
    Of sun and steel and song.

And when they came to the open land
   They wheeled, deployed, and stood;
Midmost were Marcus and the King,
And Eldred on the right-hand wing,
And leftwards Colan darkling,
   In the last shade of the wood.

But the Earls of the Great Army
   Lay like a long half moon,
Ten poles before their palisades,
With wide-winged helms and runic blades
Red giants of an age of raids,
   In the thornland of Ethandune.

Midmost the saddles rose and swayed,
   And a stir of horses' manes,
Where Guthrum and a few rode high
On horses seized in victory;
But Ogier went on foot to die,
   In the old way of the Danes.

Far to the King's left Elf the bard
   Led on the eastern wing
With songs and spells that change the blood;
And on the King's right Harold stood,
   The kinsman of the King.

Young Harold, coarse, with colours gay,
   Smoking with oil and musk,
And the pleasant violence of the young,
Pushed through his people, giving tongue
Foewards, where, grey as cobwebs, hung
   The banners of the Usk.

But as he came before his line
   A little space along,
His beardless face broke into mirth,
And he cried: 'What broken bits of earth

Are here? For what their clothes are worth
  I would sell them for a song.'

For Colan was hung with raiment
  Tattered like autumn leaves,
And his men were all as thin as saints,
  And all as poor as thieves.

No bows nor slings nor bolts they bore,
  But bills and pikes ill-made;
And none but Colan bore a sword,
  And rusty was its blade.

And Colan's eyes with mystery
  And iron laughter stirred,
And he spoke aloud, but lightly
  Not labouring to be heard.

'Oh, truly we be broken hearts,
  For that cause, it is said,
We light our candles to that Lord
  That broke Himself for bread.

'But though we hold but bitterly
  What land the Saxon leaves,
Though Ireland be but a land of saints,
  And Wales a land of thieves,

'I say you yet shall weary
  Of the working of your word,
That stricken spirits never strike
  Nor lean hands hold a sword.

'And if ever ye ride in Ireland,
  The jest may yet be said,
There is the land of broken hearts,
  And the land of broken heads.'

Not less barbarian laughter
  Choked Harold like a flood,

'And shall I fight with scarecrows
    That am of Guthrum's blood?

'Meeting may be of war-men,
    Where the best war-man wins;
But all this carrion a man shoots
    Before the fight begins.'

And stopping in his onward strides,
    He snatched a bow in scorn
From some mean slave, and bent it on
Colan, whose doom grew dark; and shone
Stars evil over Caerleon,
    In the place where he was born.

For Colan had not bow nor sling,
    On a lonely sword leaned he,
Like Arthur on Excalibur
    In the battle by the sea.

To his great gold ear-ring Harold
    Tugged back the feathered tail,
And swift had sprung the arrow,
    But swifter sprang the Gael.

Whirling the one sword round his head,
    A great wheel in the sun,
He sent it splendid through the sky,
Flying before the shaft could fly –
It smote Earl Harold over the eye,
    And blood began to run.

Colan stood bare and weaponless,
    Earl Harold, as in pain,
Strove for a smile, put hand to head,
Stumbled and suddenly fell dead;
And the small white daisies all waxed red
    With blood out of his brain.

And all at that marvel of the sword,
    Cast like a stone to slay,
Cried out. Said Alfred: 'Who would see
Signs, must give all things. Verily
Man shall not taste of victory
    Till he throws his sword away.'

Then Alfred, prince of England,
    And all the Christian earls,
Unhooked their swords and held them up,
Each offered to Colan, like a cup
    Of chrysolite and pearls.

And the King said, 'Do thou take my sword
    Who have done this deed of fire,
For this is the manner of Christian men,
Whether of steel or priestly pen,
That they cast their hearts out of their ken
    To get their heart's desire.

'And whether ye swear a hive of monks,
    Or one fair wife to friend,
This is the manner of Christian men,
    That their oath endures the end.

'For love, our Lord, at the end of the world,
    Sits a red horse like a throne,
With a brazen helm and an iron bow,
    But one arrow alone.

'Love with the shield of the Broken Heart
    Ever his bow doth bend,
With a single shaft for a single prize,
And the ultimate bolt that parts and flies
Comes with a thunder of split skies,
    And a sound of souls that rend.

'So shall you earn a king's sword,
    Who cast your sword away.'

And the King took, with a random eye,
A rude axe from a hind hard by
  And turned him to the fray.

For the swords of the Earls of Daneland
  Flamed round the fallen lord.
The first blood woke the trumpet-tune,
As in monk's rhyme or wizard's rune,
Beginneth the battle of Ethandune
  With the throwing of the sword.

BOOK VI

ETHANDUNE: THE SLAYING OF THE CHIEFS

As the sea flooding the flat sands
  Flew on the sea-born horde,
The two hosts shocked with dust and din,
Left of the Latian paladin,
Clanged all Prince Harold's howling kin
  On Colan and the sword.

Crashed in the midst on Marcus,
  Ogier with Guthrum by,
And eastward of such central stir,
Far to the right and faintlier,
The house of Elf the harp-player,
  Struck Eldred's with a cry.

The centre swat for weariness,
  Stemming the screaming horde,
And wearily went Colan's hands
  That swung King Alfred's sword.

But like a cloud of morning
  To eastward easily,
Tall Eldred broke the sea of spears
  As a tall ship breaks the sea.

His face like a sanguine sunset,
  His shoulder a Wessex down,
His hand like a windy hammer-stroke;
Men could not count the crests he broke,
  So fast the crests went down.

As the tall white devil of the Plague
  Moves out of Asian skies,
With his foot on a waste of cities
  And his head in a cloud of flies;

Or purple and peacock skies grow dark
  With a moving locust-tower;
Or tawny sand-winds tall and dry,
Like hell's red banners beat and fly,
When death comes out of Araby,
  Was Eldred in his hour.

But while he moved like a massacre
  He murmured as in sleep,
And his words were all of low hedges
  And little fields and sheep.

Even as he strode like a pestilence,
  That strides from Rhine to Rome,
He thought how tall his beans might be
  If ever he went home.

Spoke some stiff piece of childish prayer,
  Dull as the distant chimes,
That thanked our God for good eating
  And corn and quiet times –

Till on the helm of a high chief
  Fell shatteringly his brand,
And the helm broke and the bone broke
  And the sword broke in his hand.

Then from the yelling Northmen
  Driven splintering on him ran
Full seven spears, and the seventh
  Was never made by man.

Seven spears, and the seventh
  Was wrought as the faerie blades,
And given to Elf the minstrel
  By the monstrous water-maids;

By them that dwell where luridly
  Lost waters of the Rhine
Move among roots of nations,
  Being sunken for a sign.

Under all graves they murmur,
  They murmur and rebel,
Down to the buried kingdoms creep,
And like a lost rain roar and weep
  O'er the red heavens of hell.

Thrice drowned was Elf the minstrel,
  And washed as dead on sand;
And the third time men found him
  The spear was in his hand.

Seven spears went about Eldred,
  Like stays about a mast;
But there was sorrow by the sea
  For the driving of the last.

Six spears thrust upon Eldred
  Were splintered while he laughed;
One spear thrust into Eldred,
  Three feet of blade and shaft.

And from the great heart grievously
  Came forth the shaft and blade,

And he stood with the face of a dead man,
  Stood a little, and swayed –

Then fell, as falls a battle-tower,
  On smashed and struggling spears.
Cast down from some unconquered town
That, rushing earthward, carries down
Loads of live men of all renown –
  Archers and engineers.

And a great clamour of Christian men
  Went up in agony,
Crying, 'Fallen is the tower of Wessex
  That stood beside the sea.'

Centre and right the Wessex guard
  Grew pale for doubt and fear,
And the flank failed at the advance,
For the death-light on the wizard lance –
  The star of the evil spear.

'Stand like an oak, ' cried Marcus,
  'Stand like a Roman wall!
Eldred the Good is fallen –
  Are you too good to fall?

'When we were wan and bloodless
  He gave you ale enow;
The pirates deal with him as dung,
  God! are you bloodless now?

'Grip, Wulf and Gorlias, grip the ash!
  Slaves, and I make you free!
Stamp, Hildred hard in English land,
Stand Gurth, stand Gorlias, Gawen stand!
Hold, Halfgar, with the other hand,
  Halmer, hold up on knee!

'The lamps are dying in your homes,
  The fruits upon your bough;
Even now your old thatch smoulders, Gurth,
Now is the judgment of the earth,
  Now is the death-grip, now!'

For thunder of the captain,
  Not less the Wessex line,
Leaned back and reeled a space to rear
As Elf charged with the Rhine maids' spear,
  And roaring like the Rhine.

For the men were borne by the waving walls
  Of woods and clouds that pass,
By dizzy plains and drifting sea,
And they mixed God with glamoury,
God with the gods of the burning tree
  And the wizard's tower and glass.

But Mark was come of the glittering towns
  Where hot white details show,
Where men can number and expound,
And his faith grew in a hard ground
Of doubt and reason and falsehood found,
  Where no faith else could grow.

Belief that grew of all beliefs
  One moment back was blown
And belief that stood on unbelief
  Stood up iron and alone.

The Wessex crescent backwards
  Crushed, as with bloody spear
Went Elf roaring and routing,
And Mark against Elf yet shouting,
  Shocked, in his mid-career.

Right on the Roman shield and sword
  Did spear of the Rhine maids run;

But the shield shifted never,
The sword rang down to sever,
The great Rhine sang for ever,
  And the songs of Elf were done.

And a great thunder of Christian men
  Went up against the sky,
Saying, 'God hath broken the evil spear
  Ere the good man's blood was dry.'

'Spears at the charge!' yelled Mark amain,
  'Death on the gods of death!
Over the thrones of doom and blood
Goeth God that is a craftsman good,
And gold and iron, earth and wood,
  Loveth and laboureth.

'The fruits leap up in all your farms,
  The lamps in each abode;
God of all good things done on earth,
All wheels or webs of any worth,
The God that makes the roof, Gurth,
  The God that makes the road.

'The God that heweth kings in oak
  Writeth songs on vellum,
God of gold and flaming glass,
Confregit potentias
Arcuum, scutum, Gorlias,
  Gladium et bellum.'

Steel and lightning broke about him,
  Battle-bays and palm,
All the sea-kings swayed among
Woods of the Wessex arms upflung,
The trumpet of the Roman tongue,
  The thunder of the psalm.

And midmost of that rolling field
  Ran Ogier ragingly,
Lashing at Mark, who turned his blow,
And brake the helm about his brow,
  And broke him to his knee.

Then Ogier heaved over his head
  His huge round shield of proof;
But Mark set one foot on the shield,
One on some sundered rock upheeled,
And towered above the tossing field,
  A statue on a roof.

Dealing far blows about the fight,
  Like thunder-bolts a-roam,
Like birds about the battle-field,
While Ogier writhed under his shield
  Like a tortoise in his dome.

But hate in the buried Ogier
  Was strong as pain in hell,
With bare brute hand from the inside
He burst the shield of brass and hide,
And a death-stroke to the Roman's side
  Sent suddenly and well.

Then the great statue on the shield
  Looked his last look around
With level and imperial eye;
And Mark, the man from Italy,
Fell in the sea of agony,
  And died without a sound.

And Ogier, leaping up alive,
  Hurled his huge shield away
Flying, as when a juggler flings
  A whizzing plate in play.

And held two arms up rigidly,
  And roared to all the Danes:

'Fallen is Rome, yea, fallen
  The city of the plains!

'Shall no man born remember,
  That breaketh wood or weald,
How long she stood on the roof of the world
  As he stood on my shield.

'The new wild world forgetteth her
  As foam fades on the sea,
How long she stood with her foot on Man
  As he with his foot on me.

'No more shall the brown men of the south
  Move like the ants in lines,
To quiet men with olives
  Or madden men with vines.

'No more shall the white towns of the south,
  Where Tiber and Nilus run,
Sitting around a secret sea
  Worship a secret sun.

'The blind gods roar for Rome fallen,
  And forum and garland gone,
For the ice of the north is broken,
  And the sea of the north comes on.

'The blind gods roar and rave and dream
  Of all cities under the sea,
For the heart of the north is broken,
  And the blood of the north is free.

'Down from the dome of the world we come,
  Rivers on rivers down,
Under us swirl the sects and hordes
  And the high dooms we drown.

'Down from the dome of the world and down,
  Struck flying as a skiff
On a river in spate is spun and swirled
Until we come to the end of the world
  That breaks short, like a cliff.

'And when we come to the end of the world
  For me, I count it fit
To take the leap like a good river,
  Shot shrieking over it.

'But whatso hap at the end of the world,
  Where Nothing is struck and sounds,
It is not, by Thor, these monkish men
  These humbled Wessex hounds –

'Not this pale line of Christian hinds,
  This one white string of men,
Shall keep us back from the end of the world,
  And the things that happen then.

'It is not Alfred's dwarfish sword,
  Nor Egbert's pigmy crown,
Shall stay us now that descend in thunder,
Rending the realms and the realms thereunder,
  Down through the world and down.'

There was that in the wild men back of him,
  There was that in his own wild song,
A dizzy throbbing, a drunkard smoke,
That dazed to death all Wessex folk,
  And swept their spears along.

Vainly the sword of Colan
  And the axe of Alfred plied –
The Danes poured in like a brainless plague,
  And knew not when they died.

Prince Colan slew a score of them,
  And was stricken to his knee;

King Alfred slew a score and seven
  And was borne back on a tree.

Back to the black gate of the woods,
  Back up the single way,
Back by the place of the parting ways
  Christ's knights were whirled away.

And when they came to the parting ways
  Doom's heaviest hammer fell,
For the King was beaten, blind, at bay,
Down the right lane with his array,
But Colan swept the other way,
  Where he smote great strokes and fell.

The thorn-woods over Ethandune
  Stand sharp and thick as spears,
By night and furze and forest-harms
Far sundered were the friends in arms;
The loud lost blows, the last alarms,
  Came not to Alfred's ears.

The thorn-woods over Ethandune
  Stand stiff as spikes in mail;
As to the Haut King came at morn
Dead Roland on a doubtful horn,
Seemed unto Alfred lightly borne
  The last cry of the Gael.

BOOK VII

ETHANDUNE: THE LAST CHARGE

Away in the waste of White Horse Down
  An idle child alone
Played some small game through hours that pass,
And patiently would pluck the grass,
  Patiently push the stone.

On the lean, green edge for ever,
    Where the blank chalk touched the turf,
The child played on, alone, divine,
As a child plays on the last line
    That sunders sand and surf.

For he dwelleth in high divisions
    Too simple to understand,
Seeing on what morn of mystery
The Uncreated rent the sea
    With roarings, from the land.

Through the long infant hours like days
    He built one tower in vain –
Piled up small stones to make a town,
And evermore the stones fell down,
    And he piled them up again.

And crimson kings on battle-towers,
    And saints on Gothic spires,
And hermits on their peaks of snow,
    And heroes on their pyres,

And patriots riding royally,
    That rush the rocking town,
Stretch hands, and hunger and aspire,
Seeking to mount where high and higher,
The child whom Time can never tire,
    Sings over White Horse Down.

And this was the might of Alfred,
    At the ending of the way;
That of such smiters, wise or wild,
He was least distant from the child,
    Piling the stones all day.

For Eldred fought like a frank hunter
    That killeth and goeth home;

And Mark had fought because all arms
  Rang like the name of Rome.

And Colan fought with a double mind,
  Moody and madly gay;
But Alfred fought as gravely
  As a good child at play.

He saw wheels break and work run back
  And all things as they were;
And his heart was orbed like victory
  And simple like despair.

Therefore is Mark forgotten,
  That was wise with his tongue and brave;
And the cairn over Colan crumbled,
  And the cross on Eldred's grave.

Their great souls went on a wind away,
  And they have not tale or tomb;
And Alfred born in Wantage
  Rules England till the doom.

Because in the forest of all fears
  Like a strange fresh gust from sea,
Struck him that ancient innocence
  That is more than mastery.

And as a child whose bricks fall down
  Re-piles them o'er and o'er,
Came ruin and the rain that burns,
Returning as a wheel returns,
And crouching in the furze and ferns
  He began his life once more.

He took his ivory horn unslung
  And smiled, but not in scorn:
'Endeth the Battle of Ethandune
  With the blowing of a horn.'

On a dark horse at the double way
　　He saw great Guthrum ride,
Heard roar of brass and ring of steel,
The laughter and the trumpet peal,
　　The pagan in his pride.

And Ogier's red and hated head
　　Moved in some talk or task;
But the men seemed scattered in the brier,
And some of them had lit a fire,
　　And one had broached a cask.

And waggons one or two stood up,
　　Like tall ships in sight,
As if an outpost were encamped
　　At the cloven ways for night.

And joyous of the sudden stay
　　Of Alfred's routed few,
Sat one upon a stone to sigh,
And some slipped up the road to fly,
Till Alfred in the fern hard by
　　Set horn to mouth and blew.

And they all abode like statues –
　　One sitting on the stone,
One half-way through the thorn hedge tall,
One with a leg across a wall,
And one looked backwards, very small,
　　Far up the road, alone.

Grey twilight and a yellow star
　　Hung over thorn and hill;
Two spears and a cloven war-shield lay
Loose on the road as cast away,
The horn died faint in the forest grey,
　　And the fleeing men stood still.

'Brothers at arms,' said Alfred,
  'On this side lies the foe;
Are slavery and starvation flowers,
  That you should pluck them so?

'For whether is it better
  To be prodded with Danish poles,
Having hewn a chamber in a ditch,
And hounded like a howling witch,
  Or smoked to death in holes?

'Or that before the red cock crow
  All we, a thousand strong,
Go down the dark road to God's house,
  Singing a Wessex song?

'To sweat a slave to a race of slaves,
  To drink up infamy?
No, brothers, by your leave, I think
Death is a better ale to drink,
And by all the stars of Christ that sink,
  The Danes shall drink with me.

'To grow old cowed in a conquered land,
  With the sun itself discrowned,
To see trees crouch and cattle slink –
Death is a better ale to drink,
And by high Death on the fell brink,
  That flagon shall go round.

'Though dead are all the paladins
  Whom glory had in ken,
Though all your thunder-sworded thanes
With proud hearts died among the Danes,
While a man remains, great war remains:
  Now is a war of men.

'The men that tear the furrows,
  The men that fell the trees,

When all their lords be lost and dead
The bondsmen of the earth shall tread
   The tyrants of the seas.

'The wheel of the roaring stillness
   Of all labours under the sun,
Speed the wild work as well at least
   As the whole world's work is done.

'Let Hildred hack the shield-wall
   Clean as he hacks the hedge;
Let Gurth the fowler stand as cool
   As he stands on the chasm's edge;

'Let Gorlias ride the sea-kings
   As Gorlias rides the sea,
Then let all hell and Denmark drive,
Yelling to all its fiends alive,
   And not a rag care we.'

When Alfred's word was ended
   Stood firm that feeble line,
Each in his place with club or spear,
And fury deeper than deep fear,
   And smiles as sour as brine.

And the King held up the horn and said,
   'See ye my father's horn,
That Egbert blew in his empery,
Once, when he rode out commonly,
Twice when he rode for venery,
   And thrice on the battle-morn.

'But heavier fates have fallen
   The horn of the Wessex kings,
And I blew once, the riding sign,
To call you to the fighting line
   And glory and all good things.

'And now two blasts, the hunting sign,
    Because we turn to bay;
But I will not blow the three blasts,
    Till we be lost or they.

'And now I blow the hunting sign,
    Charge some by rule and rod;
But when I blow the battle sign,
    Charge all and go to God.'

Wild stared the Danes at the double ways
    Where they loitered, all at large,
As that dark line for the last time
    Doubled the knee to charge –

And caught their weapons clumsily,
    And marvelled how and why –
In such degree, by rule and rod,
The people of the peace of God
    Went roaring down to die.

And when the last arrow
    Was fitted and was flown,
When the broken shield hung on the breast,
And the hopeless lance was laid in rest,
    And the hopeless horn blown,

The King looked up, and what he saw
    Was a great light like death,
For Our Lady stood on the standards rent,
As lonely and as innocent
As when between white walls she went
    And the lilies of Nazareth.

One instant in a still light
    He saw Our Lady then,
Her dress was soft as western sky,
And she was a queen most womanly –
    But she was a queen of men.

Over the iron forest
  He saw Our Lady stand,
Her eyes were sad withouten art,
And seven swords were in her heart –
  But one was in her hand.

Then the last charge went blindly,
  And all too lost for fear:
The Danes closed round, a roaring ring,
And twenty clubs rose o'er the King,
Four Danes hewed at him, halloing,
And Ogier of the Stone and Sling
  Drove at him with a spear.

But the Danes were wild with laughter,
  And the great spear swung wide,
The point stuck to a straggling tree,
And either host cried suddenly,
  As Alfred leapt aside.

Short time had shaggy Ogier
  To pull his lance in line –
He knew King Alfred's axe on high,
  He heard it rushing through the sky,

He cowered beneath it with a cry –
  It split him to the spine:
And Alfred sprang over him dead,
  And blew the battle sign.

Then bursting all and blasting
  Came Christendom like death,
Kicked of such catapults of will,
The staves shiver, the barrels spill,
The waggons waver and crash and kill
  The waggoners beneath.

Barriers go backwards, banners rend,
  Great shields groan like a gong –

Horses like horns of nightmare
  Neigh horribly and long.

Horses ramp high and rock and boil
  And break their golden reins,
And slide on carnage clamorously,
Down where the bitter blood doth lie,
Where Ogier went on foot to die,
  In the old way of the Danes.

'The high tide!' King Alfred cried.
  'The high tide and the turn!
As a tide turns on the tall grey seas,
See how they waver in the trees,
How stray their spears, how knock their knees,
  How wild their watchfires burn!

'The Mother of God goes over them,
  Walking on wind and flame,
And the storm-cloud drifts from city and dale,
And the White Horse stamps in the White Horse Vale,
And we all shall yet drink Christian ale
  In the village of our name.

'The Mother of God goes over them,
  On dreadful cherubs borne;
And the psalm is roaring above the rune,
And the Cross goes over the sun and moon,
Endeth the battle of Ethandune
  With the blowing of a horn.'

For back indeed disorderly
  The Danes went clamouring,
Too worn to take anew the tale,
Or dazed with insolence and ale,
Or stunned of heaven, or stricken pale

Before the face of the King.
  For dire was Alfred in his hour

The pale scribe witnesseth,
More mighty in defeat was he
Then all men else in victory,
And behind, his men came murderously,
  Dry-throated, drinking death.

And Edgar of the Golden Ship
  He slew with his own hand,
Took Ludwig from his lady's bower,
And smote down Harmar in his hour,
And vain and lonely stood the tower –
  The tower in Guelderland.

And Torr out of his tiny boat,
  Whose eyes beheld the Nile,
Wulf with his war-cry on his lips,
And Harco born in the eclipse,
Who blocked the Seine with battleships
  Round Paris on the Isle.

And Hacon of the Harvest-Song,
  And Dirck from the Elbe he slew,
And Cnut that melted Durham bell
And Fulk and fiery Oscar fell,
And Goderic and Sigael,
  And Uriel of the Yew.

And highest sang the slaughter,
  And fastest fell the slain,
When from the wood-road's blackening throat
A crowning and crashing wonder smote
  The rear-guard of the Dane.

For the dregs of Colan's company –
  Lost down the other road –
Had gathered and grown and heard the din,
And with wild yells came pouring in,
Naked as their old British kin,
  And bright with blood for woad.

[143]

And bare and bloody and aloft
  They bore before their band
The body of their mighty lord,
Colan of Caerleon and its horde,
That bore King Alfred's battle-sword
  Broken in his left hand.

And a strange music went with him,
  Loud and yet strangely far;
The wild pipes of the western land,
Too keen for the ear to understand,
Sang high and deathly on each hand
  When the dead man went to war.

Blocked between ghost and buccaneer,
  Brave men have dropped and died;
And the wild sea-lords well might quail
As the ghastly war-pipes of the Gael
Called to the horns of White Horse Vale,
  And all the horns replied.

And Hildred the poor hedger
  Cut down four captains dead,
And Halmar laid three others low,
And the great earls wavered to and fro
  For the living and the dead.

And Gorlias grasped the great flag,
  The Raven of Odin, torn;
And the eyes of Guthrum altered,
  For the first time since morn.

As a turn of the wheel of tempest
  Tilts up the whole sky tall,
And cliffs of wan cloud luminous
Lean out like great walls over us,
  As if the heavens might fall.

As such a tall and tilted sky
  Sends certain snow or light,
So did the eyes of Guthrum change,
And the turn was more certain and more strange
  Than a thousand men in flight.

For not till the floor of the skies is split,
  And hell-fire shines through the sea,
Or the stars look up through the rent earth's knees,
Cometh such rending of certainties,
As when one wise man truly sees
  What is more wise than he.

He set his horse in the battle-breech
  Even Guthrum of the Dane,
And as ever had fallen fell his brand,
A falling tower o'er many a land,
But Gurth the fowler laid one hand
  Upon his bridle rein.

King Guthrum was a great lord,
  And higher than his gods –
He put the popes to laughter,
  He chid the saints with rods,

He took this hollow world of ours
  For a cup to hold his wine;
In the parting of the woodways
  There came to him a sign.

In Wessex in the forest,
  In the breaking of the spears,
We set a sign on Guthrum
  To blaze a thousand years.

Where the high saddles jostle
  And the horse-tails toss,
There rose to the birds flying
A roar of dead and dying;
In deafness and strong crying
  We signed him with the cross.

Far out to the winding river
  The blood ran down for days,
When we put the cross on Guthrum
  In the parting of the ways.

BOOK VIII

THE SCOURING OF THE HORSE

In the years of the peace of Wessex,
  When the good King sat at home;
Years following on that bloody boon
When she that stands above the moon
Stood above death at Ethandune
  And saw his kingdom come –

When the pagan people of the sea
  Fled to their palisades,
Nailed there with javelins to cling
And wonder smote the pirate king,
And brought him to his christening
  And the end of all his raids.

(For not till the night's blue slate is wiped
  Of its last star utterly,
And fierce new signs writ there to read,
Shall eyes with such amazement heed,
As when a great man knows indeed
  A greater thing than he.)

And there came to his chrism-loosing
  Lords of all lands afar,
And a line was drawn north-westerly
That set King Egbert's empire free,
Giving all lands by the northern sea
  To the sons of the northern star.

In the days of the rest of Alfred,
  When all these things were done,

[146]

And Wessex lay in a patch of peace,
  Like a dog in a patch of sun –

The King sat in his orchard,
  Among apples green and red,
With the little book in his bosom
  And the sunshine on his head.

And he gathered the songs of simple men
  That swing with helm and hod,
And the alms he gave as a Christian
Like a river alive with fishes ran;
And he made gifts to a beggar man
  As to a wandering god.

And he gat good laws of the ancient kings,
  Like treasure out of the tombs;
And many a thief in thorny nook,
Or noble in sea-stained turret shook,
For the opening of his iron book,
  And the gathering of the dooms.

Then men would come from the ends of the earth,
  Whom the King sat welcoming,
And men would go to the ends of the earth
  Because of the word of the King.

For folk came in to Alfred's face
  Whose javelins had been hurled
On monsters that make boil the sea,
Crakens and coils of mystery.
Or thrust in ancient snows that be
  The white hair of the world.

And some had knocked at the northern gates
  Of the ultimate icy floor,
Where the fish freeze and the foam turns black,
And the wide world narrows to a track,
And the other sea at the world's back
  Cries through a closed door.

And men went forth from Alfred's face,
  Even great gift-bearing lords,
Not to Rome only, but more bold,
Out to the high hot courts of old,
Of negroes clad in cloth of gold,
  Silence, and crooked swords,

Scrawled screens and secret gardens
  And insect-laden skies –
Where fiery plains stretch on and on
To the purple country of Prester John
  And the walls of Paradise.

And he knew the might of the Terre Majeure,
  Where kings began to reign;
Where in a night-rout, without name,
Of gloomy Goths and Gauls there came
White, above candles all aflame,
  Like a vision, Charlemagne.

And men, seeing such embassies,
  Spake with the King and said:
'The steel that sang so sweet a tune
On Ashdown and on Ethandune,
Why hangs it scabbarded so soon,
  All heavily like lead?

'Why dwell the Danes in North England,
  And up to the river ride?
Three more such marches like thine own
Would end them; and the Pict should own
Our sway; and our feet climb the throne
  In the mountains of Strathclyde.'

And Alfred in the orchard,
  Among apples green and red,
With the little book in his bosom,
  Looked at green leaves and said:

'When all philosophies shall fail,
  This word alone shall fit;
That a sage feels too small for life,
  And a fool too large for it.

'Asia and all imperial plains
  Are too little for a fool;
But for one man whose eyes can see
The little island of Athelney
  Is too large a land to rule.

'Haply it had been better
  When I built my fortress there,
Out in the reedy waters wide,
I had stood on my mud wall and cried:
"Take England all, from tide to tide –
  Be Athelney my share."

'Those madmen of the throne-scramble –
  Oppressors and oppressed –
Had lined the banks by Athelney,
And waved and wailed unceasingly,
Where the river turned to the broad sea,
  By an island of the blest.

'An island like a little book
  Full of a hundred tales,
Like the gilt page the good monks pen,
That is all smaller than a wren,
Yet hath high towns, meteors, and men,
  And suns and spouting whales;

'A land having a light on it
  In the river dark and fast,
An isle with utter clearness lit,
Because a saint had stood in it;
Where flowers are flowers indeed and fit,
  And trees are trees at last.

'So were the island of a saint;
   But I am a common king,
And I will make my fences tough
From Wantage Town to Plymouth Bluff,
Because I am not wise enough
   To rule so small a thing.'

And it fell in the days of Alfred,
   In the days of his repose,
That as old customs in his sight
Were a straight road and a steady light,
He bade them keep the White Horse white
   As the first plume of the snows.

And right to the red torchlight,
   From the trouble of morning grey,
They stripped the White Horse of the grass
   As they strip it to this day.

And under the red torchlight
   He went dreaming as though dull,
Of his old companions slain like kings,
And the rich irrevocable things
Of a heart that hath not openings,
   But is shut fast, being full.

And the torchlight touched the pale hair
   Where silver clouded gold,
And the frame of his face was made of cords,
And a young lord turned among the lords
   And said: 'The King is old.'

And even as he said it
   A post ran in amain,
Crying: 'Arm, Lord King, the hamlets arm,
In the horror and the shade of harm,
They have burnt Brand of Aynger's farm –
   The Danes are come again!

'Danes drive the white East Angles
  In six fights on the plains,
Danes waste the world about the Thames,
  Danes to the eastward – Danes!'

And as he stumbled on one knee,
  The thanes broke out in ire,
Crying: 'Ill the watchmen watch, and ill
  The sheriffs keep the shire.'

But the young earl said: 'Ill the saints,
  The saints of England, guard
The land wherein we pledge them gold;
The dykes decay, the King grows old,
  And surely this is hard,

'That we be never quit of them;
  That when his head is hoar
He cannot say to them he smote,
And spared with a hand hard at the throat,
  "Go, and return no more." '

Then Alfred smiled. And the smile of him
  Was like the sun for power.
But he only pointed: bade them heed
Those peasants of the Berkshire breed,
Who plucked the old Horse of the weed
  As they pluck it to this hour.

'Will ye part with the weeds for ever?
  Or show daisies to the door?
Or will you bid the bold grass
  Go, and return no more?

'So ceaseless and so secret
  Thrive terror and theft set free;
Treason and shame shall come to pass
While one weed flowers in a morass;
And like the stillness of stiff grass
  The stillness of tyranny.

[151]

'Over our white souls also
  Wild heresies and high
Wave prouder than the plumes of grass,
  And sadder than their sigh.

'And I go riding against the raid,
  And ye know not where I am;
But ye shall know in a day or year,
When one green star of grass grows here;
Chaos has charged you, charger and spear,
  Battle-axe and battering-ram.

'And though skies alter and empires melt,
  This word shall still be true:
If we would have the horse of old,
  Scour ye the horse anew.

'One time I followed a dancing star
  That seemed to sing and nod,
And ring upon earth all evil's knell;
But now I wot if ye scour not well
Red rust shall grow on God's great bell
  And grass in the streets of God.'

Ceased Alfred; and above his head
  The grand green domes, the Downs,
Showed the first legions of the press,
Marching in haste and bitterness
  For Christ's sake and the crown's.

Beyond the cavern of Colan,
  Past Eldred's by the sea,
Rose men that owned King Alfred's rod,
From the windy wastes of Exe untrod,
Or where the thorn of the grave of God
  Burns over Glastonbury.

Far northward and far westward
  The distant tribes drew nigh,

Plains beyond plains, fell beyond fell,
That a man at sunset sees so well,
And the tiny coloured towns that dwell
  In the corners of the sky.

But dark and thick as thronged the host,
  With drum and torch and blade,
The still-eyed King sat pondering,
As one that watches a live thing,
  The scoured chalk; and he said,

'Though I give this land to Our Lady,
  That helped me in Athelney,
Though lordlier trees and lustier sod
And happier hills hath no flesh trod
Than the garden of the Mother of God
  Between Thames side and the sea,

'I know that weeds shall grow in it
  Faster than men can burn;
And though they scatter now and go,
In some far century, sad and slow,
I have a vision, and I know
  The heathen shall return.

'They shall not come with warships,
  They shall not waste with brands,
But books be all their eating,
  And ink be on their hands.

'Not with the humour of hunters
  Or savage skill in war,
But ordering all things with dead words,
Strings shall they make of beasts and birds,
  And wheels of wind and star.

'They shall come mild as monkish clerks,
  With many a scroll and pen;
And backward shall ye turn and gaze,

[153]

Desiring one of Alfred's days,
  When pagans still were men.

'The dear sun dwarfed of dreadful suns,
  Like fiercer flowers on stalk,
Earth lost and little like a pea
In high heaven's towering forestry,
– These be the small weeds ye shall see
  Crawl, covering the chalk.

'But though they bridge St. Mary's sea,
  Or steal St. Michael's wing –
Though they rear marvels over us,
Greater than great Vergilius
  Wrought for the Roman king;

'By this sign you shall know them,
  The breaking of the sword,
And man no more a free knight,
  That loves or hates his lord.

'Yea, this shall be the sign of them,
  The sign of the dying fire;
And Man made like a half-wit,
  That knows not of his sire.

'What though they come with scroll and pen,
  And grave as a shaven clerk,
By this sign you shall know them,
  That they ruin and make dark;

'By all men bond to Nothing,
  Being slaves without a lord,
By one blind idiot world obeyed,
  Too blind to be abhorred;

'By terror and the cruel tales
  Of curse in bone and kin,
By weird and weakness winning,

Accursed from the beginning,
By detail of the sinning,
  And denial of the sin;

'By thought a crawling ruin,
  By life a leaping mire,
By a broken heart in the breast of the world,
  And the end of the world's desire;

'By God and man dishonoured,
  By death and life made vain,
Know ye the old barbarian,
  The barbarian come again –

'When is great talk of trend and tide,
  And wisdom and destiny,
Hail that undying heathen
  That is sadder than the sea.

'In what wise men shall smite him,
  Or the Cross stand up again,
Or charity or chivalry,
My vision saith not; and I see
No more; but now ride doubtfully
  To the battle of the plain.'

And the grass-edge of the great down
  Was cut clean as a lawn,
While the levies thronged from near and far,
From the warm woods of the western star,
And the King went out to his last war
  On a tall grey horse at dawn.

And news of his far-off fighting
  Came slowly and brokenly
From the land of the East Saxons,
  From the sunrise and the sea.

From the plains of the white sunrise,
  And sad St. Edmund's crown,
Where the pools of Essex pale and gleam
  Out beyond London Town –

In mighty and doubtful fragments,
  Like faint or fabled wars,
Climbed the old hills of his renown,
Where the bald brow of White Horse Down
  Is close to the cold stars.

But away in the eastern places
  The wind of death walked high,
And a raid was driven athwart the raid,
The sky reddened and the smoke swayed,
  And the tall grey horse went by.

The gates of the great river
  Were breached as with a barge,
The walls sank crowded, say the scribes,
And high towers populous with tribes
  Seemed leaning from the charge.

Smoke like rebellious heavens rolled
  Curled over coloured flames,
Mirrored in monstrous purple dreams
  In the mighty pools of Thames.

Loud was the war on London wall,
  And loud in London gates,
And loud the sea-kings in the cloud
Broke through their dreaming gods, and loud
  Cried on their dreadful Fates.

And all the while on White Horse Hill
  The horse lay long and wan,
The turf crawled and the fungus crept,
And the little sorrel, while all men slept,
  Unwrought the work of man.

With velvet finger, velvet foot,
  The fierce soft mosses then
Crept on the large white commonweal
All folk had striven to strip and peel,
And the grass, like a great green witch's wheel,
  Unwound the toils of men.

And clover and silent thistle throve,
  And buds burst silently,
With little care for the Thames Valley
  Or what things there might be –

That away on the widening river,
  In the eastern plains for crown
Stood up in the pale purple sky
One turret of smoke like ivory;
And the smoke changed and the wind went by,
  And the King took London Town.

(iii) POEMS (MAINLY) FOR THE *WITNESS* (CALLED THE *EYE WITNESS* FROM JUNE 1911, THE *NEW WITNESS* FROM NOVEMBER 1912.)

BALLADE D'UNE GRANDE DAME

[Published in *Poems* 1915. Fr Bernard Vaughan preached a famous series of sermons on 'the sins of society' in the Jesuit church at Farm Street in London 1906, but was well known before and after.]

Heaven shall forgive you Bridge at dawn,
The clothes you wear – or do not wear –
And Ladies' Leap-frog on the lawn
And dyes and drugs and *petits verres*.
Your vicious things shall melt in air . . .
. . . But for the Virtuous Things you do,
The Righteous Work, the Public Care,
It shall not be forgiven you.

Because you could not even yawn
When your Committees would prepare
To have the teeth of paupers drawn,
Or strip the slums of Human Hair;
Because a Doctor Otto Maehr
Spoke of 'a segregated few' –
And you sat smiling in your chair –
It shall not be forgiven you.

Though your sins cried to – Father Vaughan,
These desperate you could not spare
Who steal, with nothing left to pawn;
You caged a man up like a bear
For ever in a jailer's care
Because his sins were more than *two* . . .
. . . I know a house in Hoxton where
It shall not be forgiven you.

Envoi

Princess, you trapped a guileless Mayor
To meet some people that you knew . . .
When the last trumpet rends the air
It shall not be forgiven you.

A BALLADE OF AN ANTI-PURITAN

[Published in the *Eye Witness* 13 July, 1911.]

They spoke of Progress spiring round,
Of Light and Mrs. Humphrey Ward –
It is not true to say I frowned,
Or ran about the room and roared;
I might have simply sat and snored –
I rose politely in the club
And said, 'I feel a little bored;
Will someone take me to a pub?'

The new world's wisest did surround
Me; and it pains me to record
I did not think their views profound,
Or their conclusions well assured;
The simple life I can't afford,
Besides, I do not like the grub –
I want a mash and sausage, 'scored' –
Will someone take me to a pub?

I know where Men can still be found,
Anger and clamorous accord,
And virtues growing from the ground,
And fellowship of beer and board,
And song, that is a sturdy cord,
And hope, that is a hardy shrub,
And goodness, that is God's last word –
Will someone take me to a pub?

Envoi

Prince, Bayard would have smashed his sword
To see the sort of knights you dub –
Is that the last of them – O Lord!
Will someone take me to a pub?

THE SONG OF THE WHEELS

Written during a Friday and Saturday in August, 1911.

[That is, during a rail-strike. Published in the *Eye Witness*, 31 August 1911].

King Dives he was walking in his garden all alone,
Where his flowers are made of iron and his trees are made of stone,
And his hives are full of thunder and the lightning leaps and kills,
For the mills of God grind slowly; and he works with other mills.
Dives found a mighty silence; and he missed the throb and leap,
The noise of all the sleepless creatures singing him to sleep.
And he said: 'A screw has fallen – or a bolt has slipped aside –
Some little thing has shifted': and the little things replied:

'Call upon the wheels, master, call upon the wheels;
We are taking rest, master, finding how it feels,
Strict the law of thine and mine: theft we ever shun –
All the wheels are thine, master – tell the wheels to run!
Yea, the Wheels are mighty gods – set them going then!
We are only men, master, have you heard of men?

'O, they live on earth like fishes, and a gasp is all their breath.
God for empty honours only gave them death and scorn of death,
And you walk the worms for carpet and you tread a stone that squeals
Only, God that made them worms did not make them wheels.
Man shall shut his heart against you and you shall not find the spring.
Man who wills the thing he wants not, the intolerable thing –
Once he likes his empty belly better than your empty head
Earth and heaven are dumb before him: he is stronger than the dead.

'Call upon the wheels, master, call upon the wheels,

Steel is beneath your hand, stone beneath your heels,
Steel will never laugh aloud, hearing what we heard,
Stone will never break its heart, mad with hope deferred –
Men of tact that arbitrate, slow reform that heals –
Save the stinking grease, master, save it for the wheels.

'King Dives in the garden, we have naught to give or hold –
(Even while the baby came alive the rotten sticks were sold.)
The savage knows a cavern and the peasants keep a plot,
Of all the things that men have had – lo! we have them not.
Not a scrap of earth where ants could lay their eggs –
Only this poor lump of earth that walks about on legs –
Only this poor wandering mansion, only these two walking trees,
Only hands and hearts and stomachs – what have you to do with
       these?
You have engines big and burnished, tall beyond our fathers' ken,
Why should you make peace and traffic with such feeble folk as
       men?

'Call upon the wheels, master, call upon the wheels,
They are deaf to demagogues, deaf to crude appeals;
Are our hands our own, master? – how the doctors doubt!
Are our legs our own, master? wheels can run without –
Prove the points are delicate – they will understand.
All the wheels are loyal; see how still they stand!'

King Dives he was walking in his garden in the sun,
He shook his hand at heaven, and he called the wheels to run,
And the eyes of him were hateful eyes, the lips of him were curled,
And he called upon his father that is lord below the world,
Sitting in the Gate of Treason, in the gate of broken seals,
'Bend and bind them, bend and bind them, bend and bind them into
       wheels,
Then once more in all my garden there may swing and sound and
       sweep –
The noise of all the sleepless things that sing the soul to sleep.'

Call upon the wheels, master, call upon the wheels,
Weary grow the holidays when you miss the meals,

[161]

Through the Gate of Treason, through the gate within,
Cometh fear and greed of fame, cometh deadly sin;
If a man grow faint, master, take him ere he kneels,
Take him, break him, rend him, end him, roll him,
    crush him with the wheels.

LEPANTO

[Published in the *Eye Witness*, 7 October 1911. See Introduction. The point of the sixth verse is that seven years after the battle, King Philip procured the assassination of Don John's secretary Escovedo, and was accused of having poisoned Don John, who died later the same year. In the year of the battle he contemplated poisoning Queen Elizabeth; but Chesterton's reference to her as 'the cold queen' makes it unlikely that she is referred to here.]

White founts falling in the courts of the sun,
And the Soldan of Byzantium is smiling as they run;
There is laughter like the fountains in that face of all men feared,
It stirs the forest darkness, the darkness of his beard,
It curls the blood-red crescent, the crescent of his lips,
For the inmost sea of all the earth is shaken with his ships.
They have dared the white republics up the capes of Italy,
They have dashed the Adriatic round the Lion of the Sea,
And the Pope has cast his arms abroad for agony and loss,
And called the kings of Christendom for swords about the Cross,
The cold queen of England is looking in the glass;
The shadow of the Valois is yawning at the Mass;
From evening isles fantastical rings faint the Spanish gun,
And the Lord upon the Golden Horn is laughing in the sun.

Dim drums throbbing, in the hills half heard,
Where only on a nameless throne a crownless prince has stirred,
Where, risen from a doubtful seat and half-attainted stall,
The last knight of Europe takes weapons from the wall,
The last and lingering troubadour to whom the bird has sung,
That once went singing southward when all the world was young,
In that enormous silence, tiny and unafraid,
Comes up along a winding road the noise of the Crusade.
Strong gongs groaning as the guns boom far,
Don John of Austria is going to the war,

Stiff flags straining in the night-blasts cold
In the gloom black-purple, in the glint old-gold,
Torchlight crimson on the copper kettle-drums,
Then the tuckets, then the trumpets, then the cannon, and
    he comes.
Don John laughing in the brave beard curled,
Spurning of his stirrups like the thrones of all the world,
Holding his head up for a flag of all the free.
Love-light of Spain – hurrah!
Death-light of Africa!
Don John of Austria
Is riding to the sea.

Mahound is in his paradise above the evening star,
(*Don John of Austria is going to the war.*)
He moves a mighty turban on the timeless houri's knees,
His turban that is woven of the sunset and the seas.
He shakes the peacock gardens as he rises from his ease,
And he strides among the tree-tops and is taller than the trees,
And his voice through all the garden is a thunder sent to bring
Black Azrael and Ariel and Ammon on the wing.
Giants and the Genii,
Multiplex of wing and eye,
Whose strong obedience broke the sky
When Solomon was king.

They rush in red and purple from the red clouds of the morn,
From temples where the yellow gods shut up their eyes in scorn;
They rise in green robes roaring from the green hells of the sea
Where fallen skies and evil hues and eyeless creatures be;
On them the sea-valves cluster and the grey sea-forests curl,
Splashed with a splendid sickness, the sickness of the pearl;
They swell in sapphire smoke out of the blue cracks of the ground, –
They gather and they wonder and give worship to Mahound.
And he saith, 'Break up the mountains where the hermit-folk may
    hide,
And sift the red and silver sands lest bone of saint abide,
And chase the Giaours flying night and day, not giving rest,
For that which was our trouble comes again out of the west.

We have set the seal of Solomon on all things under sun,
Of knowledge and of sorrow and endurance of things done,
But a noise is in the mountains, in the mountains, and I know
The voice that shook our palaces – four hundred years ago:
It is he that saith not "Kismet"; it is he that knows not Fate;
It is Richard, it is Raymond, it is Godfrey in the gate!
It is he whose loss is laughter when he counts the wager worth,
Put down your feet upon him, that our peace be on the earth.'
For he heard drums groaning and he heard guns jar,
(*Don John of Austria is going to the war.*)
Sudden and still – hurrah!
Bolt from Iberia!
Don John of Austria
Is gone by Alcalar.

St. Michael's on his Mountain in the sea-roads of the north
(*Don John of Austria is girt and going forth.*)
Where the grey seas glitter and the sharp tides shift
And the sea folk labour and the red sails lift.
He shakes his lance of iron and he claps his wings of stone;
The noise is gone through Normandy; the noise is gone alone;
The North is full of tangled things and texts and aching eyes
And dead is all the innocence of anger and surprise,
And Christian killeth Christian in a narrow dusty room,
And Christian dreadeth Christ that hath a newer face of doom,
And Christian hateth Mary that God kissed in Galilee,
But Don John of Austria is riding to the sea.
Don John calling through the blast and the eclipse
Crying with the trumpet, with the trumpet of his lips,
Trumpet that sayeth ha!
   Domino gloria!
Don John of Austria
Is shouting to the ships.

King Philip's in his closet with the Fleece about his neck
(*Don John of Austria is armed upon the deck.*)
The walls are hung with velvet that is black and soft as sin,
And little dwarfs creep out of it and little dwarfs creep in.
He holds a crystal phial that has colours like the moon,

He touches, and it tingles, and he trembles very soon,
And his face is as a fungus of a leprous white and grey
Like plants in the high houses that are shuttered from the day,
And death is in the phial, and the end of noble work,
But Don John of Austria has fired upon the Turk.
Don John's hunting, and his hounds have bayed –
Booms away past Italy the rumour of his raid.
Gun upon gun, ha! ha!
Gun upon gun, hurrah!
Don John of Austria
Has loosed the cannonade.

The Pope was in his chapel before day or battle broke,
(*Don John of Austria is hidden in the smoke.*)
The hidden room in a man's house where God sits all the year,
The secret window whence the world looks small and very dear.
He sees as in a mirror on the monstrous twilight sea
The crescent of his cruel ships whose name is mystery;
They fling great shadows foe-wards, making Cross and Castle dark,
They veil the plumèd lions on the galleys of St. Mark;
And above the ships are palaces of brown, black-bearded chiefs,
And below the ships are prisons, where with multitudinous griefs,
Christian captives sick and sunless, all a labouring race repines
Like a race in sunken cities, like a nation in the mines.
They are lost like slaves that swat, and in the skies of morning hung
The stairways of the tallest gods when tyranny was young.
They are countless, voiceless, hopeless as those fallen or fleeing on
Before the high Kings' horses in the granite of Babylon.
And many a one grows witless in his quiet room in hell
Where a yellow face looks inward through the lattice of his cell,
And he finds his God forgotten, and he seeks no more a sign –
(*But Don John of Austria has burst the battle-line!*)
Don John pounding from the slaughter-painted poop,
Purpling all the ocean like a bloody pirate's sloop,
Scarlet running over on the silvers and the golds,
Breaking of the hatches up and bursting of the holds,
Thronging of the thousands up that labour under sea
White for bliss and blind for sun and stunned for liberty.
Vivat Hispania!

Domino Gloria!
Don John of Austria
Has set his people free!

Cervantes on his galley sets the sword back in the sheath
(*Don John of Austria rides homeward with a wreath.*)
And he sees across a weary land a straggling road in Spain,
Up which a lean and foolish knight forever rides in vain,
And he smiles, but not as Sultans smile, and settles back the blade. . . .
(*But Don John of Austria rides home from the Crusade.*)

ANTICHRIST, OR THE REUNION OF CHRISTENDOM: AN ODE

'A Bill which has shocked the conscience of every Christian community in Europe.' –
Mr. F. E. Smith, on the Welsh Disestablishment Bill.

[Published in the *Eye Witness*, 30 May 1912. See Introduction.]

Are they clinging to their crosses,
                    F. E. Smith,
Where the Breton boat-fleet tosses,
                    Are they, Smith?
Do they, fasting, trembling, bleeding,
     Wait the news from this our city?
Groaning 'That's the Second Reading!'
     Hissing 'There is still Committee!'
If the voice of Cecil falters,
     If McKenna's point has pith,
Do they tremble for their altars?
                    Do they, Smith?

Russian peasants round their pope
                    Huddled, Smith,
Hear about it all, I hope,
                    Don't they, Smith?
In the mountain hamlets clothing
     Peaks beyond Caucasian pales,
Where Establishment means nothing
     And they never heard of Wales,

Do they read it all in Hansard
  With a crib to read it with –
'Welsh Tithes: Dr. Clifford Answered.'
            Really, Smith?

In the lands where Christians were,
            F. E. Smith,
In the little lands laid bare,
            Smith, O Smith!
Where the Turkish bands are busy,
  And the Tory name is blessed
Since they hailed the Cross of Dizzy
  On the banners from the West!
Men don't think it half so hard if
  Islam burns their kin and kith,
Since a curate lives in Cardiff
            Saved by Smith.

It would greatly, I must own,
            Soothe me, Smith!
If you left this theme alone,
            Holy Smith!
For your legal cause or civil
  You fight well and get your fee;
For your God or dream or devil
  You will answer, not to me.
Talk about the pews and steeples
  And the Cash that goes therewith!
But the souls of Christian peoples . . .
            Chuck it, Smith!

THE SHAKESPEARE MEMORIAL

[Published 20 June 1912, *Eye Witness*.]

Lord Lilac thought it rather rotten
That Shakespeare should be quite forgotten,
And therefore got on a Committee
With several chaps out of the City,
And Shorter and Sir Herbert Tree,

Lord Rothschild and Lord Rosebery,
And F.C.G. and Comyns Carr,
Two dukes and a dramatic star,
Also a clergyman now dead;
And while the vain world careless sped
Unheeding the heroic name –
The souls most fed with Shakespeare's flame
Still sat unconquered in a ring,
Remembering him like anything.

Lord Lilac did not long remain,
Lord Lilac did not come again.
He softly lit a cigarette
And sought some other social set
Where, in some other knots or rings,
People were doing cultured things,
– Miss Zwilt's Humane Vivarium
– The little men that paint on gum
– The exquisite Gorilla Girl . . .
He sometimes, in this giddy whirl
(Not being really bad at heart),
Remembered Shakespeare with a start –
But not with that grand constancy
Of Clement Shorter, Herbert Tree,
Lord Rosebery and Comyns Carr
And all the other names there are;
Who stuck like limpets to the spot,
Lest they forgot, lest they forgot.

Lord Lilac was of slighter stuff;
Lord Lilac had had quite enough.

THE HORRIBLE HISTORY OF JONES

[Published 11 July 1912, *Eye Witness*. The author in the Isle of Wight is Tennyson.]

Jones had a dog; it had a chain;
Not often worn, not causing pain;
But, as the I.K.L. had passed

Their 'Unleashed Cousins Act' at last,
Inspectors took the chain away;
Whereat the canine barked 'hurray!'
At which, of course, the S.P.U.
(Whose Nervous Motorists' Bill was through)
Were forced to give the dog in charge
For being Audibly at Large.
None, you will say, were now annoyed,
Save haply Jones – the yard was void.
But something being in the lease
About 'alarms to aid police',
The U.S.U. annexed the yard
For having no sufficient guard;
Now if there's one condition
The C.C.P. are strong upon
It is that every house one buys
Must have a yard for exercise;
So Jones, as tenant, was unfit,
His state of health was proof of it.
Two doctors of the T.T.U.'s
Told him his legs, from long disuse,
Were atrophied; and saying 'So
From step to higher step we go
Till everything is New and True, '
They cut his legs off and withdrew.
You know the E.T.S.T.'s views
Are stronger than the T.T.U.'s:
And soon (as one may say) took wing
The Arms, though not the Man, I sing.
To see him sitting limbless there
Was more than the K.K. could bear.
'In mercy silence with all speed
That mouth there are no hands to feed;
What cruel sentimentalist,
O Jones, would doom thee to exist –
Clinging to selfish Selfhood yet?
Weak one! Such reasoning might upset
The Pump Act, and the accumulation
Of all constructive legislation;

Let us construct you up a bit –'
The head fell off when it was hit:
Then words did rise and honest doubt,
And four Commissioners sat about
Whether the slash that left him dead
Cut off his body or his head.

An author in the Isle of Wight
Observed with unconcealed delight
A land of old and just renown
Where Freedom slowly broadened down
From Precedent to Precedent . . .
And this, I think, was what he meant.

THE NEW FREETHINKER

[Published 25 July 1912, *Eye Witness*.]

John Grubby, who was short and stout
And troubled with religious doubt,
Refused about the age of three
To sit upon the curate's knee;
(For so the eternal strife must rage
Between the spirit of the age
And Dogma, which, as is well known,
Does simply hate to be outgrown).
Grubby, the young idea that shoots,
Outgrew the ages like old boots;
While still, to all appearance, small,
Would have no Miracles at all;
And just before the age of ten
Firmly refused Free Will to men.
The altars reeled, the heavens shook,
Just as he read of in the book;
Flung from his house went forth the youth
Alone with tempests and the Truth,
Up to the distant city and dim
Where his papa had bought for him
A partnership in Chepe and Deer

Worth, say, twelve hundred pounds a year.
But he was resolute. Lord Brute
Had found him useful; and Lord Loot,
With whom few other men would act,
Valued his promptitude and tact;
Never did even philanthropy
Enrich a man more rapidly:
'Twas he that stopped the Strike in Coal,
For hungry children racked his soul;
To end their misery there and then
He filled the mines with Chinamen,
Sat in that House that broke the Kings,
And voted for all sorts of things –
And rose from Under-Sec. to Sec.
With scarce a murmur or a check.
Some grumbled. Growlers who gave less
Than generous worship to success,
The little printers in Dundee,
Who got ten years for blasphemy,
(Although he let them off with seven)
Respect him rather less than heaven.
No matter. This can still be said:
Never to supernatural dread,
Never to unseen deity,
Did Sir John Grubby bend the knee;
Never did dream of hell or wrath
Turn Viscount Grubby from his path;
Nor was he bribed by fabled bliss
To kneel to any world but this.
The curate lives in Camden Town,
His lap still empty of renown,
And still across the waste of years
John Grubby, in the House of Peers,
Faces that curate, proud and free,
And never sits upon his knee.

A CIDER SONG

To J. S. M.

Extract from a Romance which is not yet written and probably never will be.

[Published in *Odd Volume*, 1912.]

The wine they drink in Paradise
They make in Haute Lorraine;
God brought it burning from the sod
To be a sign and signal rod
That they that drink the blood of God
Shall never thirst again.

The wine they praise in Paradise
They make in Ponterey,
The purple wine of Paradise,
But we have better at the price;
It's wine they praise in Paradise,
It's cider that they pray.

The wine they want in Paradise
They find in Plodder's End,
The apple wine of Hereford,
Of Hafod Hill and Hereford,
Where woods went down to Hereford,
And there I had a friend.

The soft feet of the blessed go
In the soft western vales,
The road the silent saints accord,
The road from heaven to Hereford,
Where the apple wood of Hereford
Goes all the way to Wales.

THE ARISTOCRAT

[Published 9 January 1913. *New Witness*.]

The Devil is a gentleman, and asks you down to stay
At his little place at What'sitsname (it isn't far away).
They say the sport is splendid; there is always something new,
And fairy scenes, and fearful feats that none but he can do;
He can shoot the feathered cherubs if they fly on the estate,
Or fish for Father Neptune with the mermaids for a bait;
He scaled amid the staggering stars that precipice, the sky,
And blew his trumpet above heaven, and got by mastery
The starry crown of God Himself, and shoved it on the shelf;
But the Devil is a gentleman, and doesn't brag himself.

O blind your eyes and break your heart and hack your hand away,
And lose your love and shave your head; but do not go to stay
At the little place in What'sitsname where folks are rich and clever;
The golden and the goodly house, where things grow worse for ever;
There are things you need not know of, though you live and die in vain,
There are souls more sick of pleasure than you are sick of pain;
There is a game of April Fool that's played behind its door,
Where the fool remains for ever and the April comes no more,
Where the splendour of the daylight grows drearier than the dark,
And life droops like a vulture that once was such a lark:
And that is the Blue Devil that once was the Blue Bird;
For the Devil is a gentleman, and doesn't keep his word.

WHEN I CAME BACK TO FLEET STREET

[The Chestertons had moved away from his 'jolly journalist's' life in London to Beaconsfield in Buckinghamshire in the late summer, 1909. This poem was published on 13 March 1913, in the *New Witness*.]

When I came back to Fleet Street,
   Through a sunset nook at night,
And saw the old Green Dragon
   With the windows all alight,
And hailed the old Green Dragon
   And the Cock I used to know,

[173]

Where all good fellows were my friends
     A little while ago;

I had been long in meadows,
     And the trees took hold of me,
And the still towns in the beech-woods,
     Where men were meant to be.
But old things held; the laughter,
     The long unnatural night,
And all the truth they talk in hell,
     And all the lies they write.

For I came back to Fleet Street,
     And not in peace I came;
A cloven pride was in my heart,
     And half my love was shame.
I came to fight in fairy tale,
     Whose end shall no man know –
To fight the old Green Dragon
     Until the Cock shall crow!

Under the broad bright windows
     Of men I serve no more,
The groaning of the old great wheels
     Thickened to a throttled roar:
All buried things broke upward;
     And peered from its retreat,
Ugly and silent, like an elf,
     The secret of the street.

They did not break the padlocks,
     Or clear the wall away.
The men in debt that drank of old
     Still drink in debt to-day;
Chained to the rich by ruin,
     Cheerful in chains, as then
When old unbroken Pickwick walked
     Among the broken men.

Still he that dreams and rambles
   Through his own elfin air,
Knows that the street's a prison,
   Knows that the gates are there:
Still he that scorns or struggles
   Sees, frightful and afar,
All that they leave of rebels
   Rot high on Temple Bar.

All that I loved and hated,
   All that I shunned and knew,
Clears in broad battle lightning,
   Where they, and I, and you,
Run high the barricade that breaks
   The barriers of the street,
And shout to them that shrink within,
   The Prisoners of the Fleet.

THE SONG AGAINST GROCERS

[Published in the *New Witness*, 14 November 1912.]

God made the wicked Grocer
For a mystery and a sign,
That men might shun the awful shops
And go to inns to dine;
Where the bacon's on the rafter
And the wine is in the wood,
And God that made good laughter
Has seen that they are good.

The evil-hearted Grocer
Would call his mother 'Ma'am,'
And bow at her and bob at her,
Her aged soul to damn,
And rub his horrid hands and ask
What article was next,
Though *mortis in articulo*
Should be her proper text.

His props are not his children,
But pert lads underpaid,
Who call out 'Cash!' and bang about
To work his wicked trade;
He keeps a lady in a cage
Most cruelly all day,
And makes her count and calls her 'Miss'
Until she fades away.

The righteous minds of innkeepers
Induce them now and then
To crack a bottle with a friend
Or treat unmoneyed men,
But who hath seen the Grocer
Treat housemaids to his teas

Or crack a bottle of fish sauce
Or stand a man a cheese?

He sells us sands of Araby
As sugar for cash down;
He sweeps his shop and sells the dust
The purest salt in town,
He crams with cans of poisoned meat
Poor subjects of the King,
And when they die by thousands
Why, he laughs like anything.

The wicked Grocer groces
In spirits and in wine,
Not frankly and in fellowship
As men in inns do dine;
But packed with soap and sardines
And carried off by grooms,
For to be snatched by Duchesses
And drunk in dressing-rooms.

The hell-instructed Grocer
Has a temple made of tin,
And the ruin of good innkeepers
Is loudly urged therein;
But now the sands are running out
From sugar of a sort,
The Grocer trembles; for his time,
Just like his weight, is short.

THE ENGLISHMAN

[Published 28 November 1912. *New Witness.*]

St. George he was for England,
And before he killed the dragon
He drank a pint of English ale
Out of an English flagon.
For though he fast right readily

In hair-shirt or in mail,
It isn't safe to give him cakes
Unless you give him ale.

St. George he was for England,
And right gallantly set free
The lady left for dragon's meat
And tied up to a tree;
But since he stood for England
And knew what England means,
Unless you give him bacon
You mustn't give him beans.

St. George he is for England,
And shall wear the shield he wore
When we go out in armour
With the battle-cross before.
But though he is jolly company
And very pleased to dine,
It isn't safe to give him nuts
Unless you give him wine.

THE SONG AGAINST SONGS

[Published 19 December 1912. *New Witness.*]

The song of the sorrow of Melisande is a weary song and a dreary
    song,
The glory of Mariana's grange had got into great decay,
The song of the Raven Never More has never been called a cheery
    song,
And the brightest things in Baudelaire are anything else but gay.

But who will write us a riding song
Or a hunting song or a drinking song,
Fit for them that arose and rode
When day and the wine were red?
But bring me a quart of claret out,
And I will write you a clinking song,

A song of war and a song of wine
And a song to wake the dead.

The song of the fury of Fragolette is a florid song and a torrid song,
The song of the sorrow of Tara is sung to a harp unstrung,
The song of the cheerful Shropshire Lad I consider a perfectly horrid
    song,
And the song of the happy Futurist is a song that can't be sung.

But who will write us a riding song
Or a fighting song or a drinking song,
Fit for the fathers of you and me,
That know how to think and thrive?
But the song of Beauty and Art and Love
Is simply an utterly stinking song,
To double you up and drag you down
And damn your soul alive.

THE GOOD RICH MAN

[Published 2 January 1913. *New Witness*.]

Mr. Mandragon, the Millionaire, he wouldn't have wine or wife,
He couldn't endure complexity; he lived the simple life.
He ordered his lunch by megaphone in manly, simple tones,
And used all his motors for canvassing voters, and twenty tele-
    phones;
Besides a dandy little machine,
Cunning and neat as ever was seen
With a hundred pulleys and cranks between,
Made of metal and kept quite clean,
To hoist him out of his healthful bed on every day of his life,
And wash him and brush him, and shave him and dress him to live
    the Simple Life.

Mr. Mandragon was most refined and quietly, neatly dressed,
Say all the American newspapers that know refinement best;
Neat and quiet the hair and hat, and the coat quiet and neat.
A trouser worn upon either leg, while boots adorn the feet;

And not, as any one might expect,
A Tiger Skin, all striped and flecked,
And a Peacock Hat with the tail erect,
A scarlet tunic with sunflowers decked,
– That might have had a more marked effect,
And pleased the pride of a weaker man that yearned for wine or
    wife;
But fame and the flagon, for Mr. Mandragon obscured the Simple
    Life.

Mr. Mandragon the Millionaire, I am happy to say, is dead;
He enjoyed a quiet funeral in a crematorium shed,
And he lies there fluffy and soft and grey, and certainly quite refined,
When he might have rotted to flowers and fruit with Adam and all
    mankind,
Or been eaten by wolves athirst for blood,
Or burnt on a big tall pyre of wood,
In a towering flame, as a heathen should,
Or even sat with us here at food,
Merrily taking twopenny ale and cheese with a pocket-knife;
But these were luxuries not for him who went for the Simple Life.

THE SONG OF RIGHT AND WRONG

[Published 23 January 1913. *New Witness*.]

Feast on wine or fast on water
And your honour shall stand sure,
God Almighty's son and daughter
He the valiant, she the pure;
If an angel out of heaven
Brings you other things to drink,
Thank him for his kind attentions,
Go and pour them down the sink.

Tea is like the East he grows in,
A great yellow Mandarin
With urbanity of manner
And unconsciousness of sin;
All the women, like a harem,

At his pig-tail troop along;
And, like all the East he grows in,
He is Poison when he's strong.

Tea, although an Oriental,
Is a gentleman at least;
Cocoa is a cad and coward,
Cocoa is a vulgar beast,
Cocoa is a dull, disloyal,
Lying, crawling cad and clown,
And may very well be grateful
To the fool that takes him down.

As for all the windy waters,
They were rained like tempests down
When good drink had been dishonoured
By the tipplers of the town;
When red wine had brought red ruin
And the death-dance of our times,
Heaven sent us Soda Water
As a torment for our crimes.

'THE SARACEN'S HEAD'

[Published 6 February 1913. *New Witness.*]

'The Saracen's Head' looks down the lane,
Where we shall never drink wine again,
For the wicked old women who feel well-bred
Have turned to a tea-shop 'The Saracen's Head.'

'The Saracen's Head' out of Araby came,
King Richard riding in arms like flame,
And where he established his folks to be fed
He set up a spear – and the Saracen's Head.
.   .   .   .

But the 'Saracen's Head' outlived the Kings,
It thought and it thought of most horrible things,

Of Health and of Soap and of Standard Bread,
And of Saracen drinks at the 'Saracen's Head.'

So the 'Saracen's Head' fulfils its name,
They drink no wine – a ridiculous game –
And I shall wonder until I'm dead,
How it ever came into the Saracen's Head.

THE SONG OF THE STRANGE ASCETIC

[Published 20 February 1913. *New Witness.*]

If I had been a Heathen,
  I'd have praised the purple vine,
My slaves would dig the vineyards,
  And I would drink the wine
But Higgins is a Heathen,
  And his slaves grow lean and grey,
That he may drink some tepid milk
  Exactly twice a day.

If I had been a Heathen,
  I'd have crowned Neæra's curls,
And filled my life with love affairs,
  My house with dancing girls;
But Higgins is a Heathen,
  And to lecture rooms is forced,
Where his aunts, who are not married,
  Demand to be divorced.

If I had been a Heathen,
  I'd have sent my armies forth,
And dragged behind my chariots
  The Chieftains of the North.
But Higgins is a Heathen,
  And he drives the dreary quill,
To lend the poor that funny cash
  That makes them poorer still.

If I had been a Heathen,
   I'd have piled my pyre on high,
And in a great red whirlwind
   Gone roaring to the sky.
But Higgins is a Heathen,
   And a richer man than I;
And they put him in an oven,
   Just as if he were a pie.

Now who that runs can read it,
   The riddle that I write,
Of why this poor old sinner,
   Should sin without delight –
But I, I cannot read it
   (Although I run and run),
Of them that do not have the faith,
   And will not have the fun.

WINE AND WATER

[Published 27 February 1913. *New Witness.*]

Old Noah he had an ostrich farm and fowls on the largest scale,
He ate his egg with a ladle in an egg-cup big as a pail,
And the soup he took was Elephant Soup and the fish he took was
    Whale,
But they all were small to the cellar he took when he set out to sail,
And Noah he often said to his wife when he sat down to dine,
'I don't care where the water goes if it doesn't get into the wine.'

The cataract of the cliff of heaven fell blinding off the brink
As if it would wash the stars away as suds go down a sink,
The seven heavens came roaring down for the throats of hell to
    drink,
And Noah he cocked his eye and said, 'It looks like rain, I think,
The water has drowned the Matterhorn as deep as a Mendip mine,
But I don't care where the water goes if it doesn't get into the wine.'

But Noah he sinned, and we have sinned; on tipsy feet we trod,

[183]

Till a great big black teetotaller was sent to us for a rod,
And you can't get wine at a P.S.A., or chapel, or Eisteddfod,
For the Curse of Water has come again because of the wrath of God,
And water is on the Bishop's board and the Higher Thinker's shrine,
But I don't care where the water goes if it doesn't get into the wine.

THE LOGICAL VEGETARIAN

[Published 11 September 1913. *New Witness*. See Introduction.]

'Why shouldn't I have a purely vegetarian drink? Why shouldn't I take vegetables in
their highest form, so to speak? The modest vegetarians ought obviously to stick to wine
or beer, plain vegetarian drinks, instead of filling their goblets with the blood of bulls
and elephants, as all conventional meat-eaters do, I suppose.' – *Dalroy: The Flying Inn.*

You will find me drinking rum,
　　Like a sailor in a slum,
You will find me drinking beer like a Bavarian.
　　You will find me drinking gin
　　In the lowest kind of inn,
Because I am a rigid Vegetarian.

So I cleared the inn of wine,
　　And I tried to climb the sign,
And I tried to hail the constable as 'Marion.'
　　But he said I couldn't speak,
　　And he bowled me to the Beak
Because I was a Happy Vegetarian.

Oh, I knew a Doctor Gluck,
　　And his nose it had a hook,
And his attitudes were anything but Aryan;
　　So I gave him all the pork
　　That I had, upon a fork
Because I am myself a Vegetarian.

I am silent in the Club,
　　I am silent in the pub.,
I am silent on a bally peak in Darien;

For I stuff away for life
  Shoving peas in with a knife,
Because I am at heart a Vegetarian.

  No more the milk of cows
  Shall pollute my private house
Than the milk of the wild mares of the Barbarian;
  I will stick to port and sherry,
  For they are so very, very,
So very, very, very Vegetarian.

THE ROLLING ENGLISH ROAD

[Published 25 September 1913, *New Witness*. At this time, the name of the great
London cemetery at Kensal Green had a special as well as general association for
Chesterton: the following year, when Fr O'Connor revealed to Frances that her husband
was thinking of becoming a Roman Catholic, she said that that explained his hints
about being buried at Kensal Green: the portion known as St Mary's is a probable
burying place for a Roman Catholic.]

Before the Roman came to Rye or out to Severn strode,
The rolling English drunkard made the rolling English road.
A reeling road, a rolling road, that rambles round the shire,
And after him the parson ran, the sexton and the squire;
A merry road, a mazy road, and such as we did tread
The night we went to Birmingham by way of Beachy Head.

I knew no harm of Bonaparte and plenty of the Squire,
And for to fight the Frenchman I did not much desire;
But I did bash their baggonets because they came arrayed
To straighten out the crooked road an English drunkard made,
Where you and I went down the lane with ale-mugs in our hands,
The night we went to Glastonbury by way of Goodwin Sands.

His sins they were forgiven him; or why do flowers run
Behind him; and the hedges all strengthening in the sun?
The wild thing went from left to right and knew not which was
    which,
But the wild rose was above him when they found him in the ditch.

[185]

God pardon us, nor harden us; we did not see so clear
The night we went to Bannockburn by way of Brighton Pier.

My friends, we will not go again or ape an ancient rage,
Or stretch the folly of our youth to be the shame of age,
But walk with clearer eyes and ears this path that wandereth,
And see undrugged in evening light the decent inn of death;
For there is good news yet to hear and fine things to be seen,
Before we go to Paradise by way of Kensal Green.

THE SONG OF QUOODLE

[Published 27 November 1913, *New Witness*.]

They haven't got no noses,
The fallen sons of Eve;
Even the smell of roses
Is not what they supposes;
But more than mind discloses
And more than men believe.

They haven't got no noses,
They cannot even tell
When door and darkness closes
The park a Jew encloses,
Where even the law of Moses
Will let you steal a smell.

The brilliant smell of water,
The brave smell of a stone,
The smell of dew and thunder,
The old bones buried under,
Are things in which they blunder
And err, if left alone.

The wind from winter forests,
The scent of scentless flowers,
The breath of brides' adorning,
The smell of snare and warning,

The smell of Sunday morning,
God gave to us for ours.

.　.　.　.　.

And Quoodle here discloses
All things that Quoodle can,
They haven't got no noses,
They haven't got no noses,
And goodness only knowses
The Noselessness of Man.

ME HEART

[*The Flying Inn*, 1914.]

I come from Castlepatrick, and me heart is on me sleeve,
And any sword or pistol boy can hit it with me leave,
It shines there for an epaulette, as golden as a flame,
And naked as me ancestors, as noble as me name.
For I come from Castlepatrick and me heart is on me sleeve,
But a lady stole it from me on St. Gallowglass's Eve.

The folk that live in Liverpool, their heart is in their boots;
They go to hell like lambs, they do, because the hooter hoots.
Where men may not be dancin', though the wheels may dance all
　　day;
And men may not be smokin'; but only chimneys may.
But I come from Castlepatrick, and me heart is on me sleeve,
But a lady stole it from me on St. Poleander's Eve.

The folk that live in black Belfast, their heart is in their mouth,
They see us making murders in the meadows of the South;
They think a plough's a rack, they do, and cattle-calls are creeds,
And they think we're burnin' witches when we're only burnin'
　　weeds;
But I come from Castlepatrick, and me heart is on me sleeve,
But a lady stole it from me on St. Barnabas's Eve.

WHO GOES HOME?

[*The Flying Inn*, 1914.]

In the city set upon slime and loam
They cry in their parliament 'Who goes home?'
And there comes no answer in arch or dome,
For none in the city of graves goes home.
Yet these shall perish and understand,
For God has pity on this great land.

Men that are men again; who goes home?
Tocsin and trumpeter! Who goes home?
For there's blood on the field and blood on the foam
And blood on the body when Man goes home.
And a voice valedictory . . . Who is for Victory?
Who is for Liberty? Who goes home?

IV FROM THE MARNE TO ROME
1916–1922

THE BALLAD OF ST. BARBARA

(St. Barbara is the Patron Saint of Artillery and of those in Danger of Sudden Death)

[Published 7 September 1916. *New Witness*. See Introduction.]

When the long grey lines came flooding upon Paris in the plain,
We stood and drank of the last free air we never could taste again:
They had led us back from the lost battle, to halt we knew not where
And stilled us; and our gaping guns were dumb with our despair.
The grey tribes flowed for ever from the infinite lifeless lands
And a Norman to a Breton spoke, his chin upon his hands.

'There was an end of Ilium; and an end came to Rome;
And a man plays on a painted stage in the land that he calls home;
Arch after arch of triumph, but floor beyond falling floor,
That lead to a low door at last; and beyond there is no door.'

And the Breton to the Norman spoke, like a small child spoke he,
And his sea-blue eyes were empty as his home beside the sea:
'There are more windows in one house than there are eyes to see,
There are more doors in a man's house, but God has hid the key:
Ruin is a builder of windows; her legend witnesseth
Barbara, the saint of gunners, and a stay in sudden death.'

It seemed the wheel of the world stood still an instant in its turning,
More than the kings of the earth that turned with the turning of
    Valmy mill:
While trickled the idle tale and the sea-blue eyes were burning,
Still as the heart of a whirlwind the heart of the world stood still.

   'Barbara the beautiful
   Had praise of lute and pen:
   Her hair was like a summer night
   Dark and desired of men.

   Her feet like birds from far away
   That linger and light in doubt;

And her face was like a window
Where a man's first love looked out.

Her sire was master of many slaves
A hard man of his hands;
They built a tower about her
In the desolate golden lands,

Sealed as the tyrants sealed their tombs,
Planned with an ancient plan,
And set two windows in the tower,
Like the two eyes of a man.'

Our guns were set toward the foe; we had no word, for firing.
Grey in the gateway of St. Gond the Guard of the tyrant shone;
Dark with the fate of a falling star, retiring and retiring,
The Breton line went backward and the Breton tale went on.

'Her father had sailed across the sea
From the harbour of Africa
When all the slaves took up their tools
For the bidding of Barbara.

She smote the bare wall with her hand
And bade them smite again;
She poured them wealth of wine and meat
To stay them in their pain.

And cried through the lifted thunder
Of thronging hammer and hod
"Throw open the third window
In the third name of God."

Then the hearts failed and the tools fell,
And far towards the foam,
Men saw a shadow on the sands
And her father coming home.'

Speak low and low, along the line the whispered word is flying
Before the touch, before the time, we may not loose a breath:

Their guns must mash us to the mire and there be no replying,
Till the hand is raised to fling us for the final dice to death.

    ' "There were two windows in your tower,
    Barbara, Barbara,
    For all between the sun and moon
    In the lands of Africa.

    Hath a man three eyes, Barbara,
    A bird three wings,
    That you have riven roof and wall
    To look upon vain things?"

    Her voice was like a wandering thing
    That falters yet is free,
    Whose soul has drunk in a distant land
    Of the rivers of liberty.

    'There are more wings than the wind knows
    Or eyes than see the sun
    In the light of the lost window
    And the wind of the doors undone.

    For out of the first lattice
    Are the red lands that break
    And out of the second lattice
    Sea like a green snake,

    But out of the third lattice
    Under low eaves like wings
    Is a new corner of the sky
    And the other side of things." '

It opened in the inmost place an instant beyond uttering,
A casement and a chasm and a thunder of doors undone,
A seraph's strong wing shaken out the shock of its unshuttering,
That split the shattered sunlight from a light beyond the sun.

    'Then he drew sword and drave her
    Where the judges sat and said

"Caesar sits above the gods,
Barbara the maid.

Caesar hath made a treaty
With the moon and with the sun,
All the gods that men can praise
Praise him every one.

There is peace with the anointed
Of the scarlet oils of Bel,
With the Fish God, where the whirlpool
Is a winding stair to hell,

With the pathless pyramids of slime,
Where the mitred negro lifts
To his black cherub in the cloud
Abominable gifts,

With the leprous silver cities
Where the dumb priests dance and nod,
But not with the three windows
And the last name of God." '

They are firing, we are falling, and the red skies rend and
        shiver us,
Barbara, Barbara, we may not loose a breath –
Be at the bursting doors of doom, and in the dark deliver us,
Who loosen the last window on the sun of sudden death.

'Barbara the beautiful
Stood up as queen set free,
Whose mouth is set to a terrible cup
And the trumpet of liberty.

"I have looked forth from a window
That no man now shall bar,
Caesar's toppling battle-towers
Shall never stretch so far.

The slaves are dancing in their chains,
The child laughs at the rod,
Because of the bird of the three wings,
And the third face of God."

The sword upon his shoulder
Shifted and shone and fell,
And Barbara lay very small
And crumpled like a shell.'

What wall upon what hinges turned stands open like a door?
Too simple for the sight of faith, too huge for human eyes,
What light upon what ancient way shines to a far-off floor,
The line of the lost land of France or the plains of Paradise?

'Caesar smiled above the gods
His lip of stone was curled,
His iron armies wound like chains
Round and round the world,

And the strong slayer of his own
That cut down flesh for grass,
Smiled too, and went to his own tower
Like a walking tower of brass,

And the songs ceased and the slaves were dumb
And far towards the foam
Men saw a shadow on the sands;
And her father coming home . . .

Blood of his blood upon the sword
Stood red but never dry.
He wiped it slowly, till the blade
Was blue as the blue sky.

But the blue sky split with a thunder-crack,
Spat down a blinding brand,
And all of him lay back and flat
As his shadow on the sand.'

The touch and the tornado; all our guns give tongue together
St. Barbara for the gunnery and God defend the right,
They are stopped and gapped and battered as we blast away the
  weather.
Building window upon window to our lady of the light.
For the light is come on Liberty, her foes are falling, falling,
They are reeling, they are running, as the shameful years have run,
She is risen for all the humble, she has heard the conquered calling,
St. Barbara of the Gunners, with her hand upon the gun.
They are burst asunder in the midst that eat of their own flatteries,
Whose lip is curled to order as its barbered hair is curled . . .
Blast of the beauty of sudden death, St. Barbara of the batteries!
That blow the new white window in the wall of all the world.

For the hand is raised behind us, and the bolt smites hard
Through the rending of the doorways, through the death-gap of the
  Guard,
For the cry of the Three Colours is in Condé and beyond
And the Guard is flung for carrion in the graveyard of St. Gond,
Through Mondemont and out of it, through Morin marsh and on
With earthquake of salutation the impossible thing is gone,
Gaul, charioted and charging, great Gaul upon a gun,

Tiptoe on all her thousand years and trumpeting to the sun:
As day returns, as death returns, swung backwards and swung
  home,
Back on the barbarous reign returns the battering-ram of Rome;
While that that the east held hard and hot like pincers in a forge,
Came like the west wind roaring up the cannon of St. George,
Where the hunt is up and racing over stream and swamp and tarn
And their batteries, black with battle, hold the bridgeheads of the
  Marne,
And across the carnage of the Guard, by Paris in the plain,
The Normans to the Bretons cried and the Bretons cheered
  again. . . .
But he that told the tale went home to his house beside the sea
And burned before St. Barbara, the light of the windows three,
Three candles for an unknown thing, never to come again,
That opened like the eye of God on Paris in the plain.

THE ENGLISH GRAVES

Were I that wandering citizen whose city is the world,
I would not weep for all that fell before the flags were furled;
I would not let one murmur mar the trumpets volleying forth
How God grew weary of the kings, and the cold hell in the north.
But we whose hearts are homing birds have heavier thoughts of
    home,
Though the great eagles burn with gold on Paris or on Rome,
Who stand beside our dead and stare, like seers at an eclipse,
At the riddle of the island tale and the twilight of the ships.

For these were simple men that loved with hands and feet and eyes,
Whose souls were humbled to the hills and narrowed to the skies,
The hundred little lands within one little land that lie,
Where Severn seeks the sunset isles or Sussex scales the sky.

And what is theirs, though banners blow on Warsaw risen again,
Or ancient laughter walks in gold through the vineyards of Lorraine,
Their dead are marked on English stones, their loves on English
    trees,
How little is the prize they win, how mean a coin for these –
How small a shrivelled laurel-leaf lies crumpled here and curled:
They died to save their country and they only saved the world.

THE OLD SONG

(On the Embankment in Stormy Weather)

A livid sky on London
And like the iron steeds that rear
A shock of engines halted,
And I knew the end was near:
And something said that far away, over the hills and far away,
There came a crawling thunder and the end of all things here.
For London Bridge is broken down, broken down, broken down,
As digging lets the daylight on the sunken streets of yore,
The lightning looked on London town, the broken bridge of London
    town.
The ending of a broken road where men shall go no more.

[197]

I saw the kings of London town,
The kings that buy and sell,
That built it up with penny loaves
And penny lies as well:

And where the streets were paved with gold the shrivelled paper
    shone for gold,
The scorching light of promises that pave the streets of hell.
For penny loaves will melt away, melt away, melt away,
Mock the mean that haggled in the grain they did not grow;
With hungry faces in the gate, a hundred thousand in the gate,
A thunder-flash on London and the finding of the foe.

I heard the hundred pin-makers
Slow down their racking din,
Till in the stillness men could hear
The dropping of the pin:
And somewhere men without the wall, beneath the wood, without
    the wall,
Had found the place where London ends and England can begin.
For pins and needles bend and break, bend and break, bend and break,
Faster than the breaking spears or the bending of the bow,
Of pageants pale in thunder-light, 'twixt thunderload and thunder-
    light,
The Hundreds marching on the hills in the wars of long ago.

I saw great Cobbett riding,
The horseman of the shires;
And his face was red with judgment
And a light of Luddite fires:
And south to Sussex and the sea the lights leapt up for liberty,
The trumpet of the yeomanry, the hammer of the squires;
For bars of iron rust away, rust away, rust away,
Rend before the hammer and the horseman riding in,
Crying that all men at the last, and at the worst and at the last,
Have found the place where England ends and England can begin.

His horse-hoofs go before you,
Far beyond your bursting tyres;

And time is bridged behind him
And our sons are with our sires.

A trailing meteor on the Downs he rides above the rotting towns,
The Horseman of Apocalypse, the Rider of the Shires.
For London Bridge is broken down, broken down, broken down;
Blow the horn of Huntingdon from Scotland to the sea –
... Only a flash of thunder-light, a flying dream of
    thunder-light,
Had shown under the shattered sky a people that were free.

SONGS OF EDUCATION:

III. For the crèche

[Published 25 July 1919. *New Witness.*]

Form 8277059, Sub-Section K

I remember my mother, the day that we met,
A thing I shall never entirely forget;
And I toy with the fancy that, young as I am,
I should know her again if we met in a tram.
  But mother is happy in turning a crank
  That increases the balance at somebody's bank;
  And I feel satisfaction that mother is free
From the sinister task of attending to me.

They have brightened our room, that is spacious and cool,
With diagrams used in the Idiot School,
And Books for the Blind that will teach us to see;
But mother is happy, for mother is free.
  For mother is dancing up forty-eight floors,
  For love of the Leeds International Stores,
  And the flame of that faith might perhaps have grown cold,
  With the care of a baby of seven weeks old.

For mother is happy in greasing a wheel
For somebody else, who is cornering Steel;
And though our one meeting was not very long,

She took the occasion to sing me this song:
 'O, hush thee, my baby, the time will soon come
 When thy sleep will be broken with hooting and hum;
 There are handles want turning and turning all day,
 And knobs to be pressed in the usual way;

O, hush thee, my baby, take rest while I croon,
For Progress comes early, and Freedom too soon.'

TWO POEMS ON JERUSALEM

[Frances and Gilbert Chesterton visited Jerusalem in the winter of 1919–20.
See Introduction.]

SONNET

High on the wall that holds Jerusalem
I saw one stand under the stars like stone.
And when I perish it shall not be known
Whether he lived, some strolling son of Shem,
Or was some great ghost wearing the diadem
Of Solomon or Saladin on a throne:
I only know, the features being unshown,
I did not dare draw near and look on them.

Did ye not guess . . . the diadem might be
Plaited in stranger style by hands of hate . . .
But when I looked, the wall was desolate
And the grey starlight powdered tower and tree
And vast and vague beyond the Golden Gate
Heaved Moab of the mountains like a sea.

PREFACE TO THE BALLAD OF ST. BARBARA. TO F. C.

In Memoriam Palestine, 1919.

Do you remember one immortal
Lost moment out of time and space,
What time we thought, who passed the portal
Of that divine disastrous place
Where Life was slain and Truth was slandered
On that one holier hill than Rome,
How far abroad our bodies wandered
That evening when our souls came home?

The mystic city many-gated,
With monstrous columns, was your own:
Herodian stones fell down and waited

Two thousand years to be your throne.
In the grey rocks the burning blossom
Glowed terrible as the sacred blood:
It was no stranger to your bosom
Than bluebells of an English wood.

Do you remember a road that follows
The way of unforgotten feet,
Where from the waste of rocks and hollows
Climb up the crawling crooked street
The stages of one towering drama
Always ahead and out of sight . . .
Do you remember Aceldama
And the jackal barking in the night?

Life is not void or stuff for scorners:
We have laughed loud and kept our love,
We have heard singers in tavern corners
And not forgotten the birds above:
We have known smiters and sons of thunder
And not unworthily walked with them,
We have grown wiser and lost not wonder;
And we have seen Jerusalem.

A SECOND CHILDHOOD

When all my days are ending
And I have no song to sing,
I think I shall not be too old
To stare at everything;
As I stared once at a nursery door
Or a tall tree and a swing.

Wherein God's ponderous mercy hangs
On all my sins and me,
Because He does not take away
The terror from the tree
And stones still shine along the road
That are and cannot be.

Men grow too old for love, my love,
Men grow too old for wine,
But I shall not grow too old to see
Unearthly daylight shine,
Changing my chamber's dust to snow
Till I doubt if it be mine.

Behold, the crowning mercies melt,
The first surprises stay;
And in my dross is dropped a gift
For which I dare not pray:
That a man grow used to grief and joy
But not to night and day.

Men grow too old for love, my love,
Men grow too old for lies;
But I shall not grow too old to see
Enormous night arise,
A cloud that is larger than the world
And a monster made of eyes.

Nor am I worthy to unloose
The latchet of my shoe;
Or shake the dust from off my feet
Or the staff that bears me through
On ground that is too good to last,
Too solid to be true.

Men grow too old to woo, my love,
Men grow too old to wed:
But I shall not grow too old to see
Hung crazily overhead
Incredible rafters when I wake
And find I am not dead.

A thrill of thunder in my hair:
Though blackening clouds be plain,
Still I am stung and startled
By the first drop of the rain:

Romance and pride and passion pass
And these are what remain.

Strange crawling carpets of the grass,
Wide windows of the sky:
So in this perilous grace of God
With all my sins go I:
And things grow new though I grow old,
Though I grow old and die.

VARIATIONS OF AN AIR:

Composed on Having to Appear in a Pageant as Old King Cole.

[Sold in the summer of 1920 at a bazaar for the Beaconsfield Convalescent Home,
and published in the *New Witness*, 10 December 1920.]

Old King Cole was a merry old soul,
And a merry old soul was he;
He called for his pipe,
He called for his bowl,
And he called for his fiddlers three.

After Lord Tennyson

Cole, that unwearied prince of Colchester,
Growing more gay with age and with long days
Deeper in laughter and desire of life,
As that Virginian climber on our walls
Flames scarlet with the fading of the year;
Called for his wassail and that other weed
Virginian also, from the western woods
Where English Raleigh checked the boast of Spain,
And lighting joy with joy, and piling up
Pleasure as crown for pleasure, bade men bring
Those three, the minstrels whose emblazoned coats
Shone with the oyster-shells of Colchester;
And these three played, and playing grew more fain
Of mirth and music; till the heathen came,
And the King slept beside the northern sea.

[204]

After W. B. Yeats
Of an old King in a story
  From the grey sea-folk I have heard,
Whose heart was no more broken
  Than the wings of a bird.

As soon as the moon was silver
  And the thin stars began,
He took his pipe and his tankard,
  Like an old peasant man.

And three tall shadows were with him
  And came at his command;
And played before him for ever
  The fiddles of fairyland.

And he died in the young summer
  Of the world's desire;
Before our hearts were broken
  Like sticks in a fire.

After Robert Browning
Who smoke-snorts toasts o' My Lady Nicotine,
Kicks stuffing out of Pussyfoot, bids his trio
Stick up their Stradivarii (that's the plural
Or near enough, my fatheads; *nimium*
Vicina Cremonæ; that's a bit too near).
Is there some stockfish fails to understand?
Catch hold o' the notion, bellow and blurt back 'Cole'?
Must I bawl lessons from a horn-book, howl,
Cat-call the cat-gut 'fiddles'? Fiddlesticks!

After Walt Whitman
Me clairvoyant,
Me conscious of you, old camarado,
Needing no telescope, lorgnette, field-glass, opera-glass, myopic
    pince-nez,
Me piercing two thousand years with eye naked and not ashamed;

[205]

The crown cannot hide you from me;
Musty old feudal-heraldic trappings cannot hide you from me,
I perceive that you drink.
(I am drinking with you. I am as drunk as you are.)
I see you are inhaling tobacco, puffing, smoking, spitting
(I do not object to your spitting),
You prophetic of American largeness,
You anticipating the broad masculine manners of these States;
I see in you also there are movements, tremors, tears, desire for the
      melodious,
I salute your three violinists, endlessly making vibrations,
Rigid, relentless, capable of going on for ever;
They play my accompaniment; but I shall take no notice of any
      accompaniment;
I myself am a complete orchestra.
So long.

After Swinburne

In the time of old sin without sadness
  And golden with wastage of gold
Like the gods that grow old in their gladness
  Was the king that was glad, growing old;
And with sound of loud lyres from his palace
  The voice of his oracles spoke,
And the lips that were red from his chalice
  Were splendid with smoke.

When the weed was as flame for a token
  And the wine was as blood for a sign;
And upheld in his hands and unbroken
  The fountains of fire and of wine.
And a song without speech, without singer,
  Stung the soul of a thousand in three
As the flesh of the earth has to sting her,
  The soul of the sea.

The silver and violet leopard of the night
Spotted with stars and smooth with silence sprang;
And though three doors stood open, the end of light
Closed like a trap; and stillness was a clang.

Under the leopard sky of lurid stars
I strove with evil sleep the hot night long,
Dreams dumb and swollen of triumphs without wars,
Of tongueless trumpet and unanswering gong.

I saw a pale imperial pomp go by,
Helmet and hornèd mitre and heavy wreath;
Their high strange ensigns hung upon the sky
And their great shields were like the doors of death

Their mitres were as moving pyramids
And all their crowns as marching towers were tall;
Their eyes were cold under their carven lids
And the same carven smile was on them all.

Over a paven plain that seemed unending
They passed unfaltering till it found an end
In one long shallow step; and these descending
Fared forth anew as long away to wend.

I thought they travelled for a thousand years;
And at the end was nothing for them all,
For all that splendour of sceptres and of spears,
But a new step, another easy fall.

The smile of stone seemed but a little less,
The load of silver but a little more:
And ever was that terraced wilderness
And falling plain paved like a palace floor.

Rust red as gore crawled on their arms of might
And on their faces wrinkles and not scars:

Till the dream suddenly ended; noise and light
Loosened the tyranny of the tropic stars.

But over them like a subterranean sun
I saw the sign of all the fiends that fell;
And a wild voice cried 'Hasten and be done,
Is there no steepness in the stairs of hell?'

He that returns, He that remains the same,
Turned the round real world, His iron vice;
Down the grey garden paths a bird called twice,
And through three doors mysterious daylight came.

THE SWORD OF SURPRISE

Sunder me from my bones, O sword of God,
Till they stand stark and strange as do the trees;
That I whose heart goes up with the soaring woods
May marvel as much at these.

Sunder me from my blood that in the dark
I hear that red ancestral river run,
Like branching buried floods that find the sea
But never see the sun.

Give me miraculous eyes to see my eyes,
Those rolling mirrors made alive in me,
Terrible crystal more incredible
Than all the things they see.

Sunder me from my soul, that I may see
The sins like streaming wounds, the life's brave beat;
Till I shall save myself, as I would save
A stranger in the street.

THE CONVERT

[This sonnet was written immediately after Chesterton was received into the Roman Catholic Church, 30 July 1922.]

After one moment when I bowed my head
And the whole world turned over and came upright,
And I came out where the old road shone white,
I walked the ways and heard what all men said,
Forests of tongues, like autumn leaves unshed,
Being not unlovable but strange and light;
Old riddles and new creeds, not in despite
But softly, as men smile about the dead.

The sages have a hundred maps to give
That trace their crawling cosmos like a tree,
They rattle reason out through many a sieve
That stores the sand and lets the gold go free:
And all these things are less than dust to me
Because my name is Lazarus and I live.

V LAST POEMS
1923–1933

A LITTLE LITANY

[See Introduction.]

When God turned back eternity and was young,
  Ancient of Days, grown little for your mirth
(As under the low arch the land is bright)
  Peered through you, gate of heaven – and saw the earth.

Or shutting out his shining skies awhile
  Built you about him for a house of gold
To see in pictured walls his storied world
  Return upon him as a tale is told.

Or found his mirror there; the only glass
  That would not break with that unbearable light
Till in a corner of the high dark house
  God looked on God, as ghosts meet in the night.

Star of his morning; that unfallen star
  In the strange starry overturn of space
When earth and sky changed places for an hour
  And heaven looked upwards in a human face.

Or young on your strong knees and lifted up
  Wisdom cried out, whose voice is in the street,
And more than twilight of twiformed cherubim
  Made of his throne indeed a mercy-seat.

Or risen from play at your pale raiment's hem
  God, grown adventurous from all time's repose,
Of your tall body climbed the ivory tower
  And kissed upon your mouth the mystic rose.

Our Lady went into a strange country,
   Our Lady, for she was ours
And had run on the little hills behind the houses
   And pulled small flowers;
But she rose up and went into a strange country
   With strange thrones and powers.

And there were giants in the land she walked in,
   Tall as their toppling towns,
With heads so high in heaven, the constellations
   Served them for crowns;
And their feet might have forded like a brook the abysses
   Where Babel drowns.

They were girt about with the wings of the morning and evening
   Furled and unfurled,
Round the speckled sky where our small spinning planet
   Like a top is twirled;
And the swords they waved were the unending comets
   That shall end the world.

And moving in innocence and in accident,
   She turned the face
That none has ever looked on without loving
   On the Lords of Space;
And one hailed her with her name in our own country
   That is full of grace.

Our Lady went into a strange country
   And they crowned her for a queen,
For she needed never to be stayed or questioned
   But only seen;
And they were broken down under unbearable beauty
   As we have been.

But ever she walked till away in the last high places
   One great light shone

From the pillared throne of the king of all that country
  Who sat thereon;
And she cried aloud as she cried under the gibbet
  For she saw her son.

Our Lady wears a crown in a strange country,
  The crown he gave,
But she has not forgotten to call to her old companions,
  To call and crave;
And to hear her calling a man might arise and thunder
  On the doors of the grave.

LAUGHTER

Say to the lover when the lane
Thrills through its leaves to feel her feet
'You only feel what smashed the slime
When the first monstrous brutes could meet.'
Shall not the lover laugh and say
(Whom God gives season to be gay)
'Well for those monsters long ago
If that be so; but was it so?'

Say to the mother when the son
First springs and stiffens as for fight
'So under that green roof of scum
The tadpole is the frog's delight,
So deep your brutish instincts lie.'
She will laugh loud enough and cry
'Then the poor frog is not so poor.
O happy frog! But are you sure?'

Ye learned, ye that never laugh,
But say 'Such love and litany
Hailed Isis; and such men as you
Danced by the cart of Cybele,'
Shall I not say 'Your cart at least
Goes far before your horse, poor beast

Like Her! You flatter them maybe,
What do you think you do to me?'

TRIOLET

[1928]

I wish I were a jelly fish
That cannot fall downstairs:
Of all the things I wish to wish
I wish I were a jelly fish
That hasn't any cares,
And doesn't even have to wish
'I wish I were a jelly fish
That cannot fall downstairs.'

CROOKED

[Published in *G.K.'s Weekly*, 7 September 1933.]

The little picture of the Mother of God
Hangs crooked upon the wall,
Blue and bright gold like a butterfly pinned askew,
Only it does not fall,
As, stooping ever and falling never, an eagle
Hangs winged over all.

And it suddenly seemed that the whole long room was tilted
Like a cabin in stormy seas;
The solid table and strong upstanding lamp and the inkstand
Leaned like stiff shrubs in a breeze
And the windows looked out upon slanted plains and meadows
As on slanted seas.

And I knew in a flash that the whole wide world was sliding;
Ice and not land.
And men were swaying and sliding, and nations staggered
And could not stand:
Going down to the ends of the earth, going down to destruction,
On either hand.

And knowing the whole world stiff with the crack of doom,
I pick up my pen and correct and make notes, and write small:
And go on with the task of the day, seeing unseeing
What hangs over all:
The awful eyes of Our Lady, who hangs so straight
Upon the crooked wall.

PERFECTION

[Published in *G.K's Weekly*, 16 November 1933.]

The world will not forget the weird psychological effect of the Prime Minister of Prussia shouting at a prisoner supposed to be receiving a fair trial, 'You wait till I get you outside' like a very low-class schoolboy threatening what he would do out of school. That sort of thing simply does not happen among civilised people: not even when they are very wicked people. How anybody can see such lunacy dancing in high places, in the broad daylight of political responsibility, and have any further doubt about the sort of danger that threatens the world, is more than I can understand.

Of all the heroes whom the poets sing
The one I like is General Goering:
A man of iron, cold and stern, it seems,
Ask him the simplest question and he screams,
If any other witness moves or speaks
The Court-House rings with long protracted shrieks;
These sounds, mysterious to the racial stranger,
Impress an Aryan people with the danger
Of interrupting strong and silent men
Just at the psychological moment when
They are, for Reich, Race, Goering and Gore,
Having hysterics on the Court-House floor:
Howl at us, black and purple in the face,
To note the calm of the Germanic race.
Not oft to any council, crowd or king,
Comes the high windfall of the Perfect Thing.
Those that dwell nearest Music's mightiest chords
Think the best German Songs are Without Words
Or, studying Heine's soul, may ponder long
How such a sneer became a Perfect Song:
Hitlerites may explain how Race can teach

Imperfect wits to make a Perfect Speech,
But all who know what crowns our mortal dream
Will own that Goering is a Perfect Scream.

INDEX OF FIRST LINES

[221]